USBP CAMPO & ME

JOE M. AGUILAR

To order additional copies of this book, contact:
Xlibris
844-714-8691
www.Xlibris.com
Orders@Xlibris.com

ISBN: Softcover   979-8-3694-2912-9
        Hardcover   979-8-3694-2914-3
        EBook   979-8-3694-2913-6

Library of Congress Control Number: 2024918463

Print information available on the last page

Rev. date: 09/10/2024

TABLE OF CONTENTS

INTRODUCTION

I was born in Tijuana Baja California Mexico in 1959. All my family is from a small Ranch in the state of Michoacán named San Jose de Gracia. As a child, I lived in Mexico for three years and was immigrated to the United States by my mother. Growing up I spent all my summer vacations in Mexico in that small farm town in Michoacán were all my family lives. Fortunately spending time in Mexico gave me an opportunity to speak Spanish like the natives, which was useful in my job as a border patrol agent. I attended school throughout San Diego County neighborhoods and lived-in different parts of the city. I lived for a while in the East County where I became very familiar and comfortable with the rural life. I went to college in San Diego for a while but discovered that I enjoyed working for a living better. My college education granted me the opportunity to become a United States citizen and to eventually be employed by the United States Border Patrol at the age of thirty-six. I was assigned to the Campo Border Patrol station in the east county of San Diego. I spent my entire career, all 22 years at the Campo Station. The Campo Station which is located fifty miles east of the city of San Diego in a very rural and unincorporated area. These are some of the true accounts that happened while protecting our nation's borders. Names have been changed to protect the identity of fellow border agents.

ACKNOWLEDGEMENTS

I thank all my partners in the border patrol that always had my back and helped me become one of the best agents in San Diego sector. I would also like to mention and give tribute to all the fallen agents that have given and will give their lives to protect our nation's borders. Only you that have been tasked with this can understand the true nature of the job. To all of you that know this and protect our country and Borders I dedicate this memoir. I would like to thank my family who supported me throughout my career. My wife who gave me support, motivation and unconditional love. My daughters who supported me and continue to make me proud.

HOW IT ALL STARTED

Before I was hired by the U.S. Border Patrol I was working at Home Depot. The store was a mile from my home and I had a really good shift. It began at 5:00AM and finished at 2:00PM. Monday through Friday. I was in charge of unloading big rigs with a forklift of all materials that were on a flatbed trailer. Because I spent most of the day on the forklift and was training as a power lifter in my spare time, I was at a healthy weight of 248LBS. Routinely drivers that arrived early would ask me to unload their trucks before their scheduled time. All deliveries were scheduled so I could unload the trucks in an organized manner. This meant that if I unloaded a truck before there scheduled time, I was doing the driver a favor. The drivers would win me over by buying breakfast for me.

So, as you can imagine I became very out of shape. It had been two years since I applied for a position as a Border Patrol agent but I was very comfortable with what I was doing working at Home Depot. One day I was talking to my wife and I mentioned to her that I had not heard from the hiring board about my application. My wife suggested that I call them and find out my status. I called Washington DC and spoke with a lady in the office. I explained my situation and she asked me to hold on so she could look up my information. She came back and told me that they had not received my test scores and I should fax them. I faxed my scores and a week later received the packet with all information for reporting to the Border Patrol academy. The only problem was that I would be leaving in two weeks. This meant that I had two weeks to get ready for five-months of training with very strenuous physical demands and I was not in shape. I decided to begin exercising to get in shape for the academy. I began by walking around my block at home a couple times a week and eventually got to where I could jog and not have to stop every fifty yards. I did this for a week and figured I was ready to go. The bus was waiting for us at 7:00AM at old sector headquarters on Beyer to head to the airport on our way to Georgia. The flight was all day because of the lay overs and plane transfers but we finally arrived to Savana Georgia at around 9:00PM. I was raised in San Diego all my life and when I stepped off the plane, I felt 80% humidity immediately. The humidity was so bad that it made you sweat as soon as you walked off the plane. What the hell had I got myself into? We all boarded a bus and were driven to the Federal Law Enforcement Training center in the city of Brunswick. We got to the academy around 11:00PM and were told to meet in a building to receive all our training manuals. There we received all our training manuals and a backpack that barley accommodated all our training manuals. The manuals weighed about 25lbs and we would have to carry them from class to class. We were all placed in the dorms with a roommate and were expected to report to class Monday morning. Fortunately, we arrived on a Friday and had two days to rest and prepare. While driving through the academy that night, my roommate and I noticed the obstacle course. We both agreed that we would run the course in the morning to get an idea of the physical demand. My roommate and I got up early and headed to the course to try and see what kind of time we made running the course. The first obstacle was a 7-foot inverted wall." No problem, piece of cake" I said to my roommate. "I'll go first." I got a running start and away I went. I jumped at the wall straight ahead and ended up with both elbows on top of the wall. Oh shit! I hung there for about 5 seconds and down I came. This was not a good start and as soon as my roommate saw me fail, he decided to wait on the obstacle course. The next day was the physical training evaluation which consisted of strength training, balance and agility and running. I did pretty good on the agility and balance training and was outstanding in the weight training. Prior to leaving for the academy, I was training to weight lift and was strong, I maxed out on all the weight lifting evaluations. Unfortunately, the running test was yet to come. The running portion consisted of running a mile and a half in 13 minutes or less. I knew because I didn't run often and was five foot nine and 248 pounds it was not going to be fun. We all started the run and immediately all the young guys were gone, I was left in the back with the slower runners. The run consisted of 6 laps and I was jogging pretty good but after the second lap I felt a horrible pain in my quadricep. Oh shit! I had pulled a muscle in my quad and was going to be in pain for the rest of the run. I didn't imagine that I would be running the entire time at the academy with a pulled muscle. Well, you can imagine what it was like to run every day with a pulled quadricep. Not to mention trying to keep up with the scholastics. It was very hard but I would not give up. I was 35 years old and the cutoff age was 36. There would be no way I could return to the academy in a year. At that time the academy was five months long and the mid-term there would be a pre-final PT test (Physical Training) to see where you stood. I suffered through the running, walking to class every day with a backpack full of training manuals to every class. The academy had a very good physical training center and I was instructed to go every day to receive physical therapy after class. At one point I was ready to go home, I was very discouraged. One day I called home and had a heart-to-heart talk with my cousin David. This encouraged me and motivated me to finish what I had started. At Mid-term the run was first and I was praying I would do well enough to pass. Unfortunately, I missed the time by 10 seconds (1 ½m in 13 minutes). On a positive note, I now weighed 220lbs, this made the rest of the course easier than when I got there the first day. By this time my heart was set, I was not leaving the academy without a gun and a badge. The physical therapy continued and at this point I was training PT twice a day. I decided to run with a classmate after physical training every other day to better my time. All the extra training I had done to reach this point was going to a big factor in my final exam. The day had come and I was very nervous but by now I had dropped my weight to 195lbs. I remember I only ate a muffin and a banana that morning. As it was, I had been starving myself in order to lose weight. I was in the locker room and I remember I felt sick and was very discouraged. I remember saying to God", I know you didn't bring me this far from home to fail. As we all walked out to the track It was hot and humid and again, I prayed and asked God to show me a sign, that he was there with me. My classmates and I walked out and as we got closer to the track a large black cloud came over right on top of the track. It cast a shadow over the track and a gentle breeze began. I knew then that the Lord was there with me and a sense of peace and strength flowed through me. "Ok Lord, I am ready, for I know that you are here with me and I cannot fail". We all lined up and started the run and as usual I was towards the back of the pack. I realized as I ran, I was not feeling any pain and I was invigorated by the fact that I was starting to pass people. These were the same people I had been running behind this whole time. This lifted my spirt and I began to feel I could potentially run a good time. The course was six laps or a mile and a half and I could see the fastest runners had finished. This gave me an idea of how I was doing and realized that I was on my last lap. I kept up my pace and decided that I would give it my all when I reached the half way point. As I approached the half way point, I could see three of my class mates running across the track towards me. It was Q, Fausto and Hector they had caught up to me and began to cheer me on and encourage me to run faster. This lifted my heart and spirit and I felt like the wind was pushing me towards the finish line. I crossed the finish line and heard my time. I had made the run! The emotion I felt was over whelming because I had beat the time. In addition, I had these guys that cared so much they had taken it upon themselves to run with me to the finish encouraging me to run faster the whole time. For this and for the help that I received from my Lord and Savior Jesus Christ I will always be thankful.

PURPLE THING

It was a warm morning in Campo California a community in East San Diego County in June of 1996. We all gathered for muster for our daily assignments at the Campo Border Patrol Station. Our first line Supervisor held muster and gave us our assignments, and I was assigned transport duties. Transport duties meant that I would be assigned a Ford Econoline van to be on call for agents that needed transport of undocumented aliens back to the station to be processed at a later time. Most of the shift normally would be spent driving and waiting for a call for assistance. But for me, it meant freedom to explore the area and search for undocumented aliens.

Tierra Del Sol is a paved road that runs north - south from Highway 94 near the town of Boulevard California about 7 miles long north of the United States Mexico Border. I drove south down TDS and was around the 5-mile marker driving west on the edge of the road in the eastbound lane. This enabled me to see the edge of the road and look for foot prints or any other evidence of people crossing over the road. As a (nug) new agent I really didn't know what I was doing but I was doing my best to act like it. I was looking south into a line of brush that paralleled the road and saw a purple flash of color. I didn't know what it was so I backed up and decided to take a closer look. As I approached this purple thing, I noticed it was wrapped around a lady laying on the ground. The woman was wearing a purple sweater. My first thought was, "what is this person doing out here laying on the ground". As I began to scan around the area, I noticed more people lying next to the person in purple. I immediately in my most commanding voice told them "No SE Muevan" Don't move, this would become a term used almost daily. Of course, none of them were moving or even trying to get up because they were all too busy trying to act as if I could not see them. It's funny how undocumented aliens know when you are a nug because as I stood there wide eyed looking at about 18 bodies one of the males began to stand up. Immediately I told him "No te Muevas "as he slowly got up onto one knee. I started to get a little freaked out because I thought that they would all get up and run back south to Mexico 200 yards back to the fence. I think he sensed my anxiety when I was calling for backup because no sooner had I stopped talking, he sprang up and yelled at me" Fuck You ". This got me angry and I began to chase him back south. I had taken about 4 steps when I realized that there were still a lot of illegal aliens on the ground. I stopped and returned to the group instructing them not to move or get up. I called for backup. "This is Charlie 62 I need back up on TDS near the 5-mile marker". A senior agent came on the radio and asked me "Aren't You Transport "? "Yes, and I have 18 bodies on the ground and need help walking them back to the van". The radio went silent and a short time a later the agent arrived and we loaded them into the van. I will never forget the guy that ran back south, he was a skinny young man probably in his teens with dark complexion and a leather jacket. His tactic to have me chase him and leave the group did not work but it did teach me a lesson. Don't chase the guide back south because 18 is better than nothing.

JUST IN TIME

While patrolling the Border in Tecate California with my journeyman agent on a swing shift we encountered foot prints on Emery Road. This road was commonly used by vehicles that led out of the town heading north. My journeyman was a healthy gentleman with a big appetite for pork rinds and coca cola. As we followed the footprints, I was fascinated on how easy it was to follow the foot prints from inside the vehicle. Eventually we got to a point where we were no longer able to follow the foot prints in the vehicle so we started to follow on foot. At this point I was thinking "there is no way we are going to catch up to these guys". My journeyman called to other units to get ahead of us and asked them to keep the road hot. (Drive back and forth on the road to avoid undocumented aliens from continuing north or crossing the road). We continued to walk north at a slow pace for about 2 miles. We were about 50 yards from Highway 94 and it looked like we had lost our quarry. Highway 94 is a paved road that is commonly used by smugglers to load undocumented aliens into vehicles. This further assist their entrance into the United States. We followed the foot prints to a line of brush on the side of the dirt road and sitting in the thick brush were 8 male and female subjects. We took them out of the brush and sat them on the ground next to the road. It was so interesting to me how we had followed these people for hours and finally just in the nick of time had captured them short of the area where they were going to load into a vehicle. This was a time when cell phones where not a common thing, so timing was everything to the smugglers.

CRAWLING TO SAFETY

In Tecate California the Campo Border Patrol station had an assigned fixed position just north-east of the Port of Entry. This "X" (static position) was there to show a presence in an area of the border where many Illegal aliens attempted to avoid capture every night and day. This" X" was positioned on a small hill, to the west was a flat meadow and to the east was a pond. On this day I had been assigned the X and was not supposed to work traffic or move from that spot. As I sat there contemplating what I would do if someone crossed in front of me, I noticed a young guy next to the fence. This was the smuggler guide who was watching me to see if I was alert or sleeping on my job. With the knowledge that he was watching me I did not move and stayed in the same position for what seemed like hours. Eventually he ran across the road in plain view of my vehicle and began to instruct the group he was leading to crawl on their knees across the road. Slowly the group of 15 began to crawl across the road one at a time being careful not to disturb the ground. I slowly made my way to the passenger side of the vehicle and crawled out quietly to avoiding any noise from the door or my movements. I ran north paralleling the pond on the back side of the hill to avoid detection and I positioned myself on the north west side of the pond and waited for a short time. My position gave me the advantage of seeing far enough south that I had a clear view of the edge of the pond where the group would be coming from. I allowed the them to crawl to the point where they were just below me before I stood up and told them "NO SE MUEVAN!" (Don't move). Because they had been crawling on their knees it was easy to control them except for the smuggler guide who was the last one in line. The guide ran back south cursing and screaming at me all the way to the fence. I got on my radio and asked for backup from agents. Usually, agents where not too far from the area. At that point our first line supervisor got on the radio and asked Who's on the X? I responded "I am sir", the radio went quiet, later I had to explain the reason I had left my post. This was to be a pattern that would follow me throughout my career.

TALKING TOO MUCH

It was early morning and I had just left the station on my way to Zone 27 in Tecate. Zone 27 was an area that we patrolled that covered about 10 miles east of the Tecate Port of Entry. During this time in my career, groups of undocumented aliens had routinely been crossing in the same area every morning, at about the same time. I knew that we would be notified that a group was in the area so I decided to head that way. Sure enough, as I neared the area, our dispatch notifies us of a sensor activation in the area. In the past we would set up for these groups and had good results. The exception was that we would never get the guide. With this in mind I decided to head south of the area and wait for the group. This would assist agents that apprehended aliens north of my position, just in case some of the group ran back south. I exited my vehicle and could hear the whispers of other agents on their service radios saying that they could hear the group below them. It was just a matter of time before the group would reach their position's. The group was climbing a steep incline to reach the top of a dry water fall where the agents lay in wait in the surrounding area. Suddenly all hell broke loose, agents began to yell out "No se Muevan!" Stop! I knew it wouldn't be long before I would know if any undocumented aliens had escaped and were heading my way. As it turned out the agents at the top of the waterfall had apprehended all the group except for the smuggler who had managed to again escape again. I was notified by agents who were running after the smuggler that he was running south in a deep ravine.

I knew exactly what ravine he was in because he had managed to escape in the same ravine before. I waited for short time and in the distance, I could hear the sound of someone running towards me. Because I was alone and didn't know whether or not the guide had picked up a rock or worse was armed, I drew my service issued 357 Smith and Wesson magnum and waited nervously. Suddenly he came around the corner, there he was about 20 yards away. The ravine that he had picked to make his escape was to be his unfortunate downfall on this day. The ravine was 20 feet deep and about 10 feet wide, a perfect trap. The smuggler had just now fallen into. He stopped faster than I have ever seen anybody stop, his eyes were as wide as they could possibly be as he stared at the end of my 357. I said "No Te Muevas" lay down on the ground let me see your hands and don't move. The young guide hit the ground and didn't say a thing for a short time. I holstered my weapon and hand cuffed the subject to make it harder for him to try to escape. Once he was hand cuffed the smuggler began to curse and yell obscenities at me, with no remorse. This continued all the way back to the processing center in Tecate. In those days we had a processing center in Tecate and would process all the aliens that were apprehended near the Port because of the convenience. During the processing of all the illegal aliens including the young smuggler, his foul mouth and vulgar comments continued. The guide had been separated from the rest of the group because of his attitude and was in a separate cell by himself. I opened the door to his cell and told him to be quiet several times during processing. This did not seem to faze him as he continued to curse at me and everybody else. As I approached the door for the last time to tell him to shut up, I noticed a sign that had been posted on the wall. The sign read; If any smuggler guides or persons of interest are arrested notify Groupo BETA. Groupo BETA at that time was kind of like the Border Patrol in Mexico, except for the fact that they did not wear uniforms or patrol the border consistently. I opened the cell door and told the smuggler "Hey stop your yelling and shit talking or I'm going to call Groupo BETA and tell them to meet at the port. The guide started laughing and began to say really bad things about Groupo BETA. At that point I was done with this guy and closed the door. I picked up the telephone and dialed the number that was posted for notifications to Groupo BETA. To my surprise Agent Rodriguez answered the call in a deep and scruffy voice. "Digame" (Tell Me). "Yes Sir" I said (Si Senior). I am agent Aguilar from the United States Border Patrol and I would like to turn in a guide that we have apprehended. "Oh SI" (Oh Yea). Yes Sir, and just to let you know he has been saying some pretty bad things about you guys. "OH si" (Oh yeah). He has been saying that all of you guys are a bunch of fat ice cream vendors (Paleteros) and do nothing but get fat all day. Furthermore, he said really bad things about your mothers "Chingen Su Madre" and that he would bone all you and your daughters. "OH SI!". The more I explained to him what had been said the angrier he became.

Finally, he had enough and spoke. "Ok we will be waiting for him". "Ok I will be taking all the subjects back in about 20 minutes" I said. I finished processing all the illegal aliens and opened the door to the cell where the smuggler was being held. Immediately he began to talk shit to me, and I let him know that I had spoken with Groupo BETA and that they would be waiting for him at the port. The guide turned white as a ghost and began to cry. "Please Sir" "don't be mean I was only joking; I didn't mean anything by what I was saying, please". I closed the door and really didn't think he was being sincere because of the way he had been acting. I finished processing the illegal aliens and loaded all of them into a van for their return to Mexico. The last one to get loaded in the van was the guide. I walked up to the door and noticed that the guide was still sobbing. "Come on let's go (Vamonos) don't be a crybaby, those guys will probably not even be there" I said. I loaded him in the van and drove to the Tecate Port of Entry. As I approached the drop off area, I noticed in the distance two heavy set gentlemen in plain clothes. I stopped the van and unloaded the illegal aliens one at a time. I pointed toward Mexico and instructed them to start walking. The last one to get out of the van was the guide. As soon as the guide saw two guys in Mexico waiting, he grabbed the side of the van and would not let go. It took a lot to pry him off and walk him towards the border where the two guys were waiting. There is a line painted on the sidewalk at the Port that indicates the border between Mexico and the United States. I reached the line dragging him and turned him over to the two guys. "Groupo BETA?" "Si Senor" here is your man. Immediately they grabbed the smuggler by the hair and began to repeat all the names that he had called them. As I left, I could hear punches that may or may not have been impacts being given to the guide. As I drove away, I could see in my rear-view mirror the two men dragging him back further into Mexico.

FOGG SUCKS

On the midnight shift agents were assigned from early evening to early morning, this made for a long night of patrolling the border. On this particular night I was assigned to patrol the border east of the Tecate Port Entry. It was a cold and foggy night with very poor visibility, downright creepy. I never did like the fog and would prefer to work in any other type of weather. It made me nervous and tense because you couldn't see a damn thing in front of you. The border fence was about five feet away and you could barely see it through the fog. As I drove east from the port down the road a sensor activation was relayed to me from dispatch. I responded and let dispatch know that I would be in the area shortly. I arrived in the area and exited my vehicle; it was quiet and cold and I began to walk up the trail where the sensor was located. I could only see about five feet in front of me and knew that the border was about 20 yards behind me. This made the whole situation more stressful. I finally arrived to the right location and noticed foot prints in the soft moist soil of about maybe one or two guys. I continued to investigate the foot prints and focused all my attention on the ground. I was having trouble figuring out which way these guys were going. It looked like they were going both ways, north and south. I walked up north for a bit and then turned around and began to walk back south. Suddenly I felt like I was not alone. I hadn't heard anything so this made me even more nervous. I slowly turned around and standing about five feet away from me was a young man, just staring at me. I yelled out "Hey, no te muevas"" (don't move!) loud enough so that the citizens of Tecate probably heard me. Of course, the guy was just standing there not moving. I asked him what the hell are you doing sneaking up on me like that. All this time holding the grip to my service weapon. In a soft quite voice he said I'm lost and don't where I am. I grabbed him and put him in cuffs and asked him if there was anybody else out here with him. He said he was alone and had been walking up and down the trail for many hours. I loaded him in my vehicle and took him in for processing. Damn I hate fog.

HITCH HIKER

It was another day on patrol in Campo's area of responsibility as I traveled westbound towards Tecate California. As I began to drop into Bell Valley on highway 94, I could see at a far distance a person standing on the edge of the road. Bell Valley is a deep valley on highway 94 that is about ¾ of a mile long on a two-lane highway. As I drove closer to the person on the side of the road, I could see that it was a woman. I slowed down to investigate and could see as I got closer the lady was dirty and had brush in her hair. I exited my vehicle and began to talk to her as she brushed herself off. I asked her what she was doing out here in the middle of nowhere. Her answer was that she was waiting for her vehicle. I asked her where her vehicle was coming from and she said "De aya" (From over there) Due to the fact that she was all dirty and had tumble weeds in her hair, I asked if she had any immigration documents. She said she did but not on her and that they "were at her home. "Ok where do you live?" No answer. "How did you get here? "" I was walking the road" (Caminando) she said. As I began to look around, I noticed that something had slid down the steep cutbank that was right next to us. She continued to say that she had documents and that her vehicle would be there soon. Not realizing as she was talking to me, she turned and exposed a big rip down her pants. Obviously, this had been caused by her sliding down the cutbank on her ass. I said to her "ma'am" (Senora) You have a big rip on the back of your pants. Furthermore, I can see that someone slid down this hill right to the spot where you were standing. She smiled and continued to pull weeds out of her hair. Again, I asked her again if she had any documents and she said she didn't. I loaded her into the vehicle, notified dispatch that I was transporting a female and continued on my way to Tecate.

THE BIG BUSH

For week's illegal aliens had been crossing in the same area on the road in zone 27, on the south side of a ridge named Brush Draggers. There was a road that made a complete circle around the top of the ridge called the Skeet Range Road. On this particular day I decided to go to the road and lay in wait on the south side of the loop, for UDA's (undocumented aliens) that were crossing early in the morning. I positioned myself on the east side of the loop so that I could see anything crossing the road to the west of me. I had just gotten comfortable in a cluster of boulders that gave me a real good view, but yet kept me hidden. Just then a sensor was activated. This sensor happened to be just south of the road and west of my position. It usually took groups about 5 to 10 minutes to get to the road once they activated the sensor. I waited, and waited and waited, until finally I was like, these guys should have popped out on the road by now. I got up and looked around to see if maybe they had gone further west and were trying to cross the road somewhere else. "Nah", why would they do that if the road was so close? I decided I would go to the trail they would be on to see what was going on. I looked at the trail and there were no foot prints there. I started walking south on the trail for about 25 yards and when I looked up, there they were, right in front of me. It was about 15 or so, we all froze for a second and then all hell broke loose. They all turned around and began to run back on the trail with me right behind them. The trail was a windy path that was surrounded by brush that eventually came over the top of a large cap rock. Of course, by now, the group was getting further away because I was trying to be careful not fall or hurt myself as I ran across this large rock. I was almost to the end of the rock when I heard a familiar sound. It sounded like metal clanging. I continued to run a for a few more steps when suddenly I realized, because I reached down and felt my holster, that my Smith and Wesson 357 magnum had fallen out of my holster. I immediately stopped and turned around in a panic to try to find my weapon. Because at this point, I didn't care about the UDA's. I was just worried about finding my gun. I searched frantically for my gun trying to figure out about where I had lost it. Finally, I found my gun laying just off the cap rock in the brush. I contemplated just leaving and moving on because by now the UDAs were probably way south getting close to the border. "Well,", I said "what the hell I'll just take my time and track these guys south make sure they are going back". I began to try to track the group and was having a hell of a time staying on the foot prints. NUG! Eventually I lost the foot prints so I began to look around in the bushes or anywhere else they could hide. As I was looking around, I looked in this one large bush and could see a weird color, inside the middle of it (People?). I was about 50 yards from it so I decided I would tactically move toward the bush trying to avoid being seen by the UDAs. It took me a while to move from bush to bush tactfully to get close enough to the bush. At this point I was about 20 yards from the bush peeking from behind a large bush. The strange color was still there and tried to see what was inside the center of this large bush. This whole time I thought that it was the group that had eluded me hiding in the bush. Well, here we go! I jumped from behind my cover with my gun in my hand and ran as fast as I could, yelling "Don't move, let me see your hands". It seemed like it took me forever to get to the bush but I finally made it. "No se muevan" "DON'T Move!" I panned around gun in hand expecting them to move. No movement. What the hell? No movement! I moved some low hanging branches to get further in the center of the bush and at that point realized that it was not the group I had chased earlier. It looked like a bunch of old clothes that someone had thrown away. By now my adrenaline had calmed and I began to laugh at myself for having been so careful in approaching this bush. As I stared at what I thought were clothes I noticed some yellow nylon rope on top of the green bags. "BAG's!" it wasn't clothes it was bags! Five large military style bags with yellow nylon rope tied to the top of them. "Holy shit! I got bags!" My excitement quickly went away when I realized I was alone, in the middle of nowhere with title 21 (Marijuana) and 15 UDAs possibly in the area. I drew my gun again and stood at the ready as I called for backup on my hand-held radio. "I got bags in zone 27, anybody copy" I must have sounded nervous because shortly after my classmate answered up. "Where you at Joe?" I nervously gave him a description of my location and told him to bring more agents to help with the bags. Eventually they came including my classmate and we carried all 5 bags out of the area and back to the station. It was mid-summer and it was probably 100 degrees in the shade. Carrying those damn bags was a bitch especially as hot as it was and the trail was straight up. Needless to say, we were all done when we got all the bags back to the vehicles. When we got to the station, we weighted the bags and the total weight was 385 pounds. Of course, until now the story was that I was actively pursuing a group back south when my keen eye noticed bags under a large bush.

ONE EYED GUIDE

Once again, I found myself in zone 27 sitting on a large boulder looking west towards the skeet range road early in the morning. I had a clear view of the road below me anxiously waiting for a group to cross at any moment. In recent days we had been apprehending groups of undocumented aliens that were being led by a one-eyed guide who was using this route and always managed to get away. As I sat there, I was thinking what a cool job getting paid to be out in the country enjoying a beautiful view and a beautiful morning. Then sure enough a sensor activation was relayed by our dispatch. This sensor was located just south of the road and it usually took groups about 10 minutes to get to the road. Just as I expected a group of about 15 came walking out of the brush heading towards the road. The guide was in front of the group as they approached the edge of the road. As I watched, I could see him signal the group to stop just short of the road. He carefully walked closer to the road and began to stare at the ground. I suddenly remembered that when I got there in the morning, I had walked the road from my position west and back to make sure there had not been any crossings. Now I realized that he had saw my foot prints.

The smuggler pointed at the ground as he began to instruct the group to go back the way they had come. "Shit!" I watched as the group disappeared back into the brush. I watched the road for about 5, to 10, 15 minutes. All this time expecting to see the group cross the road in a different spot. Now I began to feel stressed because I knew the group had crossed the road and I had missed them. Now they had a 15-minute lead on me. I jumped out of my high point and began to walk the road looking for any sign of the group crossing. As I reached a rocky part the road, I noticed a brush out (brush dragged used to cover foot prints) on the south side of the road on a small trail. I walked it south a bit and noticed foot prints heading north on the trail. I knew it was the group so I turned around and walked back. When I got back to the road I looked and discovered that there was no way I could see this spot from where I had been. I smiled, realizing this guide pretty damn good. I studied the road and noticed that there were no foot prints on the road. "Hum!" I walked across the road and I noticed another brush out on the north side of the road. I walked it a little further and there they were, the same foot prints that were on the south side. I began to stare at the road to try to figure out what the group had done to cross the road and not leave any evidence. Then I saw a rock the size of a melon, but flat, had been dislodged from its original position in the dirt. The constant impact and movement of the rock had made a 1-inch gap all the way around it. It was apparent to me that the group individually had jumped from the edge of the road on to the rock, which was about right in the middle of the road jumped to the north side of the road without leaving a mark. Wow! this guide has skills. I began to follow the foot prints once more that were heading north towards highway 94.

From where I was, I could see the road about two hundred yards away and I had lost this group for the time being. I thought to myself "Aww what the hell I'll Walk these guys out to see where they crossed the road". I could see highway from where I was standing. I got on the radio and advised my partners I would be out to highway 94 shortly. I continued to walk and came to a large cap rock. "Shit! "The cap rock very big, so big it was possible that a group could hide in any of the large cracks that were in this rock. I decided I would start by looking around the edge of the cap rock. Maybe I could see where they had jumped off the rock. As I walked toward the east edge of the rock, I caught I familiar smell coming from a large crack right in front of me. It was that distinct smell of burnt firewood. Illegal aliens spend a lot of time around fire camp which saturates their clothes with smell of smoke. I slowly approached the large crack and I could see individuals lying in the cracks. I got on the radio and let my partners know that I had bodies and my location. My back up arrived and we began to pull the bodies out of the cracks. We had reached the end of our search and I realized that we were missing the guide. I began to question the men in the group asking about the guide that had allowed them to get caught. I looked at one guy and he gave me a sideways nod of the head. I headed in the direction that he had nodded and found a small crack about the size of a bath tub. It was odd because it was the only crack that I saw that had a big piece of brush in it. As I looked closer at the bush, I could see something that looked like an eye in one of the gaps in the bush. I grabbed the bush and pulled it out of the crack, and there lying in the crack was a guy staring at me with one eye. I told him to get out and of and he acted as if he was invisible. Finally, after some persuasive words, he crawled out "Como estas "how you doing? I said to the smuggler. Not one word was spoken by the guy. I knew this was the guide I had seen earlier on the road with the group. "Ok, this adventure is over for you" and we loaded them all into the van and transported them back to the station.

SMALL BRUSH OUT

As I was driving eastbound on the "G" road in Zone 27 near Tecate, I came across a small bush out (a manor to conceal foot prints) across the dirt road. Staring at dirt roads along the border to try and find any kind of evidence of a group (undocumented aliens) that had crossed the road, is what we did on a daily basis. I got out of my vehicle and began to study the ground trying to figure out what I had in front of me. I could tell that something or somebody had left some scratches all the way across the road. After a few minutes I could tell that someone had used a piece brush to disguise any foot prints on the road. What was really strange is that this brush out was really narrow. Usually brush outs were wide, to disguise foot prints of large groups that crossed the road. I got on the radio and told my partners what I had saw and that I would be starting to follow the foot prints. As I began to follow the group, I explained to my partners the direction they were heading. I told them to drive the Skeet range road to see if there was any foot sign on the road. As I followed the group, I was having a hard time figuring out how many of them there were and what if any foot prints were visible. Adding to this, agents kept asking me how many was there and what type of foot prints where being left behind. I was kind of new at this (Nug) I wasn't too sure of how many I was following. I was catching a glimpse of a Converse type tennis shoe every now and then and a Running "W". Eventually an agent reached the Skeet range road and began to look for the foot prints. He said "Do you have a cowboy boot?" foot print? "I said "well I'm not sure they are not leaving very much", "How many do you think you're following?" I didn't want to sound dumb so I guessed "ten". He said "well there is nothing but old foot prints up here, so I don't know". I said "Ok well I'm heading towards you so just keep looking please". By the sound of the agent, I could tell he was doubting me and my abilities. Of course, he purposely said everything on the radio so everyone could hear our conversation. I thought to myself "What a Dick" I continued to follow the foot prints and finally reached a point just short of the Skeet range road. The agent radioed "Do you have anything out, I'm almost out to the road". "No, just old shit" he said. "Ok, I just hit the road and there are foot prints all over the road. The radio went quiet. As I continued to follow the group north on the Skeet range road, I noticed an agent with a cowboy hat standing on a large boulder directly in front me. "Hey bro the group is heading right towards you" I said to him. At this time, we were getting swamped daily by large groups and losing hundreds daily. In an attempt to assist us we were getting detailed agents from other sectors to help us. The Texas agents wore straw cowboy hats and boots and were easy to recognize. "I don't see anybody and I've been up here for a little bit," said the Texan. As I continued the foot prints of the group started to move away from his location. I was just 25 yards below Texan agent, "Hey bro there right here, do you want to follow them

from here "I said. "No not me he said you do your thing; I'll just keep an eye on you from here." "Ok."
By now I realized that there was more than the ten I was following but still not able to say exactly how
many. There was a shit load! As I began to walk, I could hear vehicles arriving near my location and
agents talking in the distance. I took a few more steps and could see the top of people's heads strung
out in a long row right in front of me in the brush. "Hey Bro! there right here!" I yelled at the Texan.
"Ok send them up! From where I was standing, I could see about ten maybe more, I wasn't quite sure.
"Ok, let's go, get up" I said to the group in Spanish as they stared at me wondering where the hell I
had come from. I had to repeat myself several times, each time louder," let's go, get up, move!" To my
surprise the group began to get up and as they did there were bodies spread out all over the place. At
this point I ran down the same path that they had taken trying to get to the end of the group. I got on
the radio and began to tell the agents above me that there was a bunch of UDAs down where I was. I
waited a bit and when I was able to see agents starting down towards me, I began to send the UDA's
up towards the agents. Slowly the group began to walk towards the agent and as they did, I begin to
count them. Ten, twenty, thirty, forty, forty-two. Forty-two UDAs came out of the brush to everyone's
surprise, including myself. As we waited for transport several agents began to lay in on the agent that
had been a "Dick ". "Old sign it looks pretty good to me" said a journeyman standing near buy. "Damn
good tracking if you ask me" said the Texan as he grabbed another UDA and placed him in the van.

CLEANING LADY

On a hot summer night on a midnight shift I was assigned to an "X" (static position) in Zone 27 near Tecate California. This particular X was just west of Crouches Pond on a small hill that overlooked the POE to the east. There was a sensor at that time near the fence that let us know if somebody had entered or attempted to enter the United States near the there. I listened to the alert from our dispatch and noticed that the sensor had only been called out for a single strike. This meant to me that there was a possibility it may not be good or just some kind of animal. "10-4, 820" I said. I waited for a while and slowly made my way down towards the border to check the sensor. I arrived at the area of the sensor activation and noticed that it was a pair, two sets of footprints heading north. I got on the radio and advised some of my fellow agents that I had checked the sensor and it was good for a pair heading north. I began to follow the footprints and I eventually was about a mile north of the border. There I met up with an agent and we began to track the pair towards a trailer up on a hill. As we got closer, I could see a guy standing outside a trailer pointing north and saying "They went that way". Funny thing, it was two o'clock in the morning and he was outside watering and racking his driveway. The footprints I had followed from the border were at this point heading right up his drive way to the trailer.

He continued to yell with an excited voice "they went that way!" I said "Ok" and we continued to follow the foot prints that led directly to his front door. At this point the man had stepped onto a set of stairs that led into the trailer. "US Border Patrol sir! how are you doing tonight?" I spoke. "Fine, a little while ago some guys were walking that way" (as he pointed to the north) towards some bushes. "Oh yea?" I spoke. "Well, I've been following these footprints for an hour from the border and they stop right here. The man stopped talking. "It looks to me that they lead right into your trailer". No response from the man. "Is this your trailer?" I asked "Jess" the man responded. How many people are inside the trailer? "There are three people inside, my wife and my son and me. Oh, ok well, I have tracks that lead right to your door. Can I come in and check to make sure there is nobody in here that you don't know? "Weeellll", at that point I was on the stairs that lead into the trailer and could see a person laying on the floor in the middle of the living room. Who is that? I asked. As I pointed at the person on the floor. As I walked in, I noticed a lady sitting in the kitchen trying to hide her face, with her hands. I also noticed a stove that had some carne asada and refried beans in a pan sitting on the burners. I really didn't focus on the lady sitting there at that time but noticed her still hiding her face. I walked further into the trailer and approached a young boy lying on the floor watching TV.

I asked the man of the house who the boy was and he answered "That's my son". As I moved towards the center of the trailer I looked to the left and could see into a small bedroom. On the bed in this room was a young man. I said to the man "You said there was only three people in here, who is this?" as I pointed towards the young man. "I don't know" the man said. I walked into the room and as I approached the young man, I could see a plate of food sitting on a dresser right next to him. It was a plate of carne asada and beans. At this point I knew the young man had been given food and was being aided by the people in the trailer. Immediately I asked the young man on the bed "Where is the other guy?" He looked at me with a defeated look and motioned towards a closed door next to the bed. I opened the door to a small bathroom and there sitting on the toilet was the second man I had been following from the border. I grabbed him by his wrist and walked him and handcuffed them to each other. As I began to walk them out of the trailer, I was able to get a good look at the lady that had been sitting at the kitchen table. To my surprise it was the Campo station cleaning lady, who had been hired to clean the station during the week. "Hey that is the cleaning lady! I yelled. My partner looked and verified that it was her. We called for a supervisor and waited for him to arrive. He arrived and we filled him in on all that had transpired. He instructed us to take the UDAs in for further processing and said he would call intel to handle the rest. We never did see the cleaning lady back at the Campo station again.

DRUNK GUIDE ON TRACKS

I was still a trainee riding with a journeyman partner in Zone 27 east of Tecate on midnight shift. Dispatch informed us that a sensor had been activated near the little trestle. It was about 5 minutes down and my journeyman informed me that we were close. My partner we would lay in wait for the group on the rail road tracks. My journeyman explained that the group would be walking the tracks right to us. He said that we would take them lights out (flash lights off) to avoid them from busting (scattering all over) everywhere. Barnie also said that we would hear the tracks snap long before the group got to us. That sounded odd but whatever he was the journeyman. He advised other agents that we would be laid in wait ready to apprehend the group and would alert them as to when to come in and assist us.

The plan was that Barnie would stop the group and that I should fall in behind them once they all passed my location. I began to think about what he had said and knowing that his Spanish wasn't as good as mine, I asked him if I could stop the group. He paused for a moment then agreed to let me stop the group. I told him I would take the group down lights out and would let him know when to come out. He didn't say anything and just walked away; he was probably thinking "look at this Fucken trainee telling me what to do". I had already decided what I was going to do, now it was just a matter of doing it. I settled into my spot and sure enough the rail road tracks began to snap. It wasn't long before I could hear people walking down the tracks heading right for us. It was really dark and I was accustomed to wearing a black beanie which hid my face. I wasn't too worried about my uniform being it was so dark. The group came closer and closer until finally the lead guy was right in front of me. I stood up quietly and began to whisper in Spanish to him. "Hey, hey calmados sientense la migra esta aqui enfrente esperandonos todos sientense.". "Hey, hey calm down sit down the border patrol is right in front of us waiting for us." To my surprise everybody sat down as well. The guide stopped but could not see who I was so he sat down. I sat next to him and asked him if there were any more people coming and he said "Un Chingo!" (a bunch). I slowly walked to the end of the group and called out for Barnie. The rest of the group had sat down when they saw the guide and everybody else sit on the ground. At this point there was about 15 in sitting on the tracks. Barnie came out of the brush behind the group and I told him to go to the front of the group so that I could stop the next group. "No se muevan somos migra!" I said" Don't move we are Border patrol". At this point the group realized they had been tricked and began to talk and grumble about being caught. "There's more coming Barnie let's do the same thing again".

Barnie sat in the front of the group while I sat at the end next to the last guy waiting for more people. Sure, enough the tracks began to snap again. As we waited the group began to talk loudly laughing and joking knowing that the next group would be next in the trap. "Hey calmados, callense" "hey calm down and be quiet" I said to the group. Soon after that I heard the next group walking towards us. I used the same tactic again and sat the group down on the tracks and slowly walked to the end of the group. Now we had about 30 subjects sitting on the tracks. Again, I asked the last guy at the end of the group if there were more coming and he said yes. Barney and I set up our trap again. I tried to keep the group quiet, because by now we had about 30 joking and laughing at our tactic to apprehend the groups. I hid next to the tracks, got on my knees and waited for the next group arrive. I heard them coming before I could see the silhouette of a guy wrapped in a blanket walking towards me. As he got close, I stood up and gave him the same line about the Border Patrol being up ahead and waited for his reaction. The guide stopped and began to say "A mi me vale madre la migra vamonos!" "Fuck the migra lets go." At this point I noticed the strong odor of alcohol coming from his breath and knew who I was dealing with. It was a drunk Tecate guide that was working in our AOR (area of responsibility).

The reason we knew it was him was because He always left empty Tecate beer cans on the trail when he would guide groups north. At that point I knew the conversation was over so I grabbed him and slammed him to the ground. "Hijo de la chingada que te pasa!" "Son of a bitch what's the matter with you!" he yelled as he attempted to get up off the ground. Callate y no te muevas buey soy la migra!" "Shut up idiot and don't move I am the border patrol!" Seeing this the group immediately sat down thinking he was sitting them down. At this point we called in the other agents that were really close to us as we took control of the group of 48. The group was relatively cool except for the drunk guide who realized the gig was up and wanted to fight. Agents arrived and we took them all into custody. This tactic was one of many that enabled me to arrest many UDA's during my career.

HORIZON VIEW
LESSON LEARNED

It was a day shift and I was riding with a journeyman agent in Zone 27. He was about a month ahead of me so he really wasn't that crusty like the older guys. Anyway, we were assigned to zone 27 Tecate and were heading towards Highway 188, when dispatch informed us of a sensor activation near Horizon view. We responded and informed that we would head that way and check it out. On the way over there, my partner was telling me how he had put in the sensor where it was and it would take the group about 20 minutes to get to the road. It was a long straight dirt road with several large dips surrounded by open fields. The timing was going to be close but we both knew we had enough time to get there. Finally, we arrived to and began to drive down the dirt road. As we drove, we began to formulate a possible plan that would enable us to catch as many undocumented aliens as possible. As we were talking and driving, I noticed a large group of people dropping into one the large dips on the road. "Hey bro is that them?" I asked. As we both looked down the road, we both realized that there were people as far as you could see walking the road towards us. There were about fifty of them just walking right down the middle of the road. My partner said nothing and accelerated the vehicle towards as I grabbed the door handle to get ready to jump out. At this point the group spotted us and began to scatter in all directions "Their Busting!" We finally got close and we both jumped out trying to grab whoever was closest to the vehicle. I ran after a group of four but was only able to catch a fat guy that hurt his ankle. I dragged him back to the vehicle while he was complaining that he couldn't walk because he had twisted his ankle. I sat the old man down next to our vehicle and told him not to move. Thinking that he was injured I began to look around for other people I could apprehend. I met up with my partner and I noticed that he had not caught one single guy. "What happened Bro?" I asked "Man, they busted everywhere and in this open field forget it bro!" he said. We both laughed and began to walk back to the vehicle. "How many did you get?" he asked. "I got one bro, the old hurt guy!" We both began to laugh again and finally made our way back to our vehicle. "Yea he's right, shit, he's gone bro!" I yelled, as I looked around frantically. "That bastard! He said he was hurt so I left him here!" Man, he acted like he could barely walk and he's gone. We both began to laugh as we realized that we had both been boned by the group of 50 and had nothing to show for it. Well shit its late in the shift and this group will regroup later, so we can just pass this on the next shift. We both agreed and returned back to the station to tell our tale to the rest of the agents. It was a lesson well learned about how you can be deceptive but you can be deceived as well.

SOMETHING NOT RIGHT

As I evolved as a Border Patrol agent, I was assigned trainees to show them the area and teach them the little bit I had learned in the short time I was in service. One day, after a strong rain in zone 28 near Tecate I decided to head to an area known as the grease Pit. The Grease Pit was a ranch east of Tecate that was a recycling site for used grease from local restaurants. As it turned out it was a cover for a smuggling organization that would smuggle, aid and abet illegal aliens throughout the year. On this particular day I knew, as we all knew, that there would be a lot of bodies in the area of the Grease Pit. During the rain aliens would use the abandoned vehicles on the property to take cover from the rain. The road that led to the ranch, was a windy dirt road that was on the side of a mountain, that opened up to a large clearing where all the buildings were. On the way up the hill, I was telling Manny my partner that because of the heavy rain there would probably be a lot of aliens all over the ranch. My intent was to drive directly to an area where there were a bunch of abandoned vehicles, and as I got closer, I noticed a little girl riding a bike in her front yard. As soon as she saw us, she threw her bike down and ran into a dilapidated trailer. That just did not seem right and before we could get out of our vehicle a lady came running out with the little girl dragging behind. They both jumped in a car and sped off like a bat out hell. Manny and I looked at each other and smiled as we watched her speed away. I began to look around a and noticed a large Conex box next the trailer which was where they had been, so close together you couldn't walk between the trailer and the box. We walked up to the Conex and I immediately noticed that an attempt was made to sweep the area right in front of the container. It was very obvious because nothing else had been swept in the area except in front of the Conex box. The Conex had no doors. I looked inside I could see that somebody had put a large piece of plywood across the front of it as if to keep something in or keep something out. The closer I got to the entrance the more I could smell burned firewood. This smell came from the aliens because they were always around camp fires and carried that smell with them everywhere they went. I looked into the rear of the Conex Box and was having problems getting a good look inside. I could see something that looked like a person, way in the back. I slid the plywood over just enough to squeeze through and turned my stinger (small flashlight) on to get a better view. At this point I could see what appeared to be a large pile of clothes and miscellaneous junk stacked all over the place. As I walked closer to the pile of clothes, I noticed something move, so I stopped and said (No se Muevan!") don't move! No sooner had I spoke when a guy threw a blanket covering him and raised his hands. Seeing this I yelled at him to stand up and keep his hands up. To my surprise when I said this about ten more people stood up with their hands up. "Oh shit! Manny!" I called," hey bro I've got aliens in here bro! Manny came running in and flashed his light at the group at the same time telling them" No se muevan!". Don't move! We both decided we would take them out individually with one of us outside the Conex and the other inside. One by one I instructed them to get up and move outside after a quick search. Manny searched them a second time outside just to make sure. Finally, we had got them all out of the Conex and had 15 aliens on the ground. "Damn Bro" I said" this is the first place we've looked". Manny just smiled as if we had just completed a mission with great results. I said "Ok Bro, let's keep looking around" We called for transport and secured the aliens we had in custody before we began to look for more. We both walked to an old station wagon that was near the trailer and tried to look inside. Obviously, it hadn't ran for years, it had no wheels and was a rust bucket. Other than that, it had all its four doors and windows and would provide a good place to be out of the rain. We each took a side of the station and began looking inside attempting to open the doors. Looking through the windows all you could see was a big pile of clothes, lying in the car. Eventually, Manny got one of the doors open and began to move the clothes around with his baton. "I don't see anything Bro" he said. Just as he said that he moved a piece of clothes and I could see a shoe with a foot in it. "Body Bro" I said as he stopped to look at me. I opened the opposite side of the door and grabbed the foot "No se Mueva!" don't move I said. I pulled on the foot and from the pile of clothes popped a skinny guy. We kept moving clothes around and found two other guys. Then we found another two guys and a girl. We eventually ended up with 6 more aliens from that old station wagon. We secured the six and noticed a large milk truck not too far from where we were. It was an old dairy milk truck that would make deliveries to your house and had those old crates to carry the milk in. Manny stayed with the aliens and I walked over to have a closer look.

I noticed that the truck had two back doors that were locked and a sliding door in the front passengers' side. I grabbed the handle and it opened right up. There was no one in the front compartment but there was another sliding door that led to back of the truck. I gave it a tug it didn't open and finally after a few harder tugs it did. There on the floor of the truck lay a young girl and a guy laying on a bunch of old clothes, wearing nothing but their underwear. Immediately I noticed that the young girl seemed to be really scared and shaking. I asked them both if they were ok because they were both wet and it was cold. I asked the young girl who the guy was and he blurted out I'm her husband. "Hey I'm talking to her!" I said "So! I'm her husband!" he said in Spanish. I knew he was the Fucken guide, due to his attitude. He had separated himself from the group with a young girl. "Ok" I said as I grabbed him stood him up and cuffed him. "Vamos a ver buey" I said Well see dude as I dragged him out of the truck. We located an old blanket and wrapped the young girl in it and gathered all the others together to transport them back to the station. Transport arrived and we returned back to the Campo. At the station we interviewed the young girl and it was no surprise that the dude was not her husband. After several attempts to convince her, she would be safe to tell us if had molested her she would not say anything. The guide would instill so much fear into our victims they refused to say anything. Anytime we suspected that it had happened to girls or guys this was the same result. We notified the sheriff and they said they needed to have her admit to a crime in order to continue the investigation. This happened frequently.

GOOD MORING SENIOR

Early on a Midnight shift a sensor went off near the intersection of Round Potrero Road and Potrero Valley Road in Zone 27. I responded dispatch (820) and advised that I would be heading to the area. This sensor had been placed recently on a two-track dirt road in the middle of a large field. I really didn't know how long it would take the group to get to the road so I rushed to get there before they did. I got out of my vehicle and started walking south on the road looking for foot sign (prints) to let my partners know what I was seeing. I came to a point where I could see foot prints that indicated that a large group had come to this point and turned around. I began to walk south and started to hear the sound of people breaking brush up a big mountain. I located where the group had scurried up the mountain. I followed the foot sign and eventually started climbing up the mountain behind the group. As I made my way up the mountain, I could tell it was a big group just by all the disturbance they were leaving behind. I kept climbing and could hear some people way up the hill and a few right above me. As I made my way up, I would stop and let the agents know my position and get a quick rest. I finally was able to catch a few aliens that got tired and gave up half way up the mountain. This was a tactic used by the guides to salvage most of the group and sacrifice a few of the slower ones. Luck was on my side because by the time the five or six guys that gave up stopped, I was exhausted. I could barely talk and told them not to move and to show me their hands. I caught my breath turned around and realized at this point that I was way up the side of this mountain. As I looked down towards the road, I could see a single vehicle rolling to a stop way down below me. "Whoever is in that vehicle, I'm up here, see my light? "I said as I shined my flashlight at them. "10-4", said a familiar voice" I'll be right there". "Hey bro, I've got six on the ground and the rest aren't stopping", I'll start to make my way down just give me a minute. As I was saying this, I could see a single agent climbing up the mountain at a pretty fast pace right towards me. "Hey bro did you copy?" I asked. There was no stopping Gus, this is how he worked. He was the type of agent that would do anything to help his fellow agents. I knew that before too long he would be up to me and so I waited for him to make his way up. When he finally reached my location, he had a big smile on his face. He asked me how many did I think where in the group. I told him that my best guess would be about 20. "Ok", let me look for some more further up and I'll let you know what's up". "Ok" I said as I watched his light disappear into the dark side of the mountain. It seemed like a long time but eventually Gus came back with three more aliens and we started to make or way. "Hey bro what do you think" Gus said as we slowly made our way down. "Well, I think we should leave the rest of the group alone and let them regroup" "Eventually they will pop up somewhere and we can work them where it's easier'. "Yea ok", said Gus. "I'll come back later and make some cuts further north. He knew locations where they had popped out in the past. "Ok" We called for transport and loaded the bodies (aliens) into the van and as we were loading them another sensor went off near Tecate. "Let's go" we both said as we jumped into our vehicles. The night continued with group after group being worked and eventually Gus and I got separated. Eventually, there was a gap in the night and I was able to return to the area of the first group that we had worked at the beginning of our shift. It was almost sunrise and I had finished looking in every spot where I believed the earlier group would at some point be out. "Damn, nothing", I said as I thought about what my next move would be. Well, I'm going to go back and see if I can figure out what they did. I returned to the area where we had walked the group out to the road and to my surprise "Damn! ". There was the foot sign right on top of us, the whole group. Apparently, the group had waited for us to leave, regrouped and popped out to the road, walking all over the top of our foot prints. I got on the radio and called Gus and said "Gus's copy, the group is out to the road bro". "I'm going to try to find where the foot sign leads from here and I'll let you know what's going on Gus responded" "10-4, I'll start rolling your way".

Because I had already looked north for the group, I knew that they had to be between where I was and the next road north about half a mile or so away. I began to follow the foot sign and noticed it was a large group. "Hey Gus, it's our guys from earlier and it's a bunch!" "Which way they going "asked Gus. "Straight north right now but I'll let you know. Hey, I already cut up (looked for foot sign) north and they weren't out" so if you want to start cutting again for these guys that would be great. I walked up a small path for about 5 minutes when I noticed a very large oak tree right in the middle of the trail in a large field. I was staring at this oak tree with admiration, because of its thick trunk and hadn't noticed a guy laying right in the middle of the trail. I could hardly believe it was a person but as I got closer, I could see it was a young man asleep on the dirt path. I quietly walk up on him and woke him up. "No te muevas calmado" Don't move relax, I told the guy as he slowly came out of his deep sleep. "Hey donde estan los de mas?" Hey where are the rest? "I asked the guy. He shrugged his shoulders and said "No se, yo me perdi y aqui me quede toda la noche'. I don't know, I got lost and stayed here all night". "Ok vamonos" Ok let's go. At this point I had a feeling that the tree I had been looking at would a perfect place to hide. I radioed to Gus and told him what had transpired and told him that I would let him know if I found anything under that big oak. I slowly and quietly walked up to the oak tree but before I could get there, I again got that strong odor of burnt firewood. The aliens were all under the tree asleep. At this point I couldn't radio Gus because I was too close to the group and didn't want to wake them up. I grabbed the guy I found on the trail and sat him down with his legs spread apart right next a group of about six guys that were laying close to each other. One by one I began to wake them up. "Hey senor," I whispered to the first guy. "No te muevas'. My gun pointed at the guy's face, "migra". Because there was about 20 or more people laying around at the base of this tree and I was alone, I figured this was the safest way for me to apprehend as many of these guys as I could without risking my safety. A guy woke to see a Smith and Wesson 357 magnum gun barrel in his face and said nothing. I grabbed him and sat him down between the first guy's legs and told the second guy to lay back against the first guys chest. This was a tactic that made it very difficult for either one of them to get up. One by one and using this tactic I continued to gain control of the group. Finally, a couple guys began to wake up but by the time they realized what was going on I had them sitting between one of their companions' legs. Eventually I had them and could control them if needed because they were only a few feet apart." Hey Gus copy, I have the rest of the group 10-15 (apprehended) bro, there's about 28 ""10-4, where are you?" asked Gus. At this point the sun had come up and I could see Round Potrero road. As I waited for Gus to show up, I stopped to look around this giant tree again. I was surprised because while looking around, I noticed a guy crouched down grabbing his knees staring right at me. We both looked at each other for a bit and then he slowly got up and walked away. It was kind of creepy because I hadn't known he was there. How long had he been there? Why didn't he wake up the group by yelling or had he just woken up? This was obviously the guide. I watched him walk away and tried to remember his face just in case we ever met again. "Hey Gus, just drive down Round P and I'll let you know where to stop". I didn't have to wait long when I heard a vehicle turn onto Round P and head towards me. "Stop, Stop I yelled on my radio". I can see your vehicle back up a little bit and I'll call your stop". "10 -4", answered that familiar voice. Gus backed up and I told him to stop. He was straight in sight from where I was standing. "I'm right here bro see my light?" :10-4" Ok Gus if you walk east there is wire gap you can go through, get on that trail and you will walk right up to me". Before I could say anything else I could hear the sound of breaking brush and bamboo. Gus had got out of his vehicle and ran straight towards me with no disregard for the creek that was between us. It didn't take long and he was standing right next to me with a big smile on his face. "Good job Joe! good job" he said several times. This is the group that got away, earlier, right? "Yea bro this is them". There are twenty-eight. Well twenty-nine if you count the one that got away. "What?" Gus said. Yea the guide got away, but we will get another chance no worries. We rounded up the group and called for transport. This is only one of the many times that I had the great privilege to work with such a special agent like Gus. Not only was he my partner he was my very good friend.

BROKEN FLASHLIGHT

Again, I found myself in Zone 28 working traffic (looking for Undocumented aliens) that had crossed through a tunnel. These groups usually headed for highway 94 towards the little trestle. A sensor was activated near the tunnel so I responded and decided to go in at Dog Patch. I let my partners know that I would be lying in wait (laid in) and would let them know when to come in or what to do. There was an old barbwire fence line that paralleled the tracks that I could walk next to. I found a large bush that was next to the fence and laid in waiting for the group. It usually took groups about 15 minutes to get to this point and I was there in plenty of time. I sat down and waited and could hear the tracks below me snap. The group was on their way. The area I had stopped to lay in was a 40-foot cut bank that was on the side of the tracks. The groups had begun taking this route because they had gotten tired of getting boned (apprehended) on the tracks. I figured the group would not run down the steep bank and the fence line would keep them from running north. Groups usually walked on the south side of the fence. As I was laying there in the pitch dark, I marveled at all the stars I could see and how many there were. Suddenly I could hear footsteps coming towards me at a distance. I sat up and positioned myself, ready to pounce. Then I realized, the group was walking the north side of the fence line not the south! Shit! I slowly began to try to crawl through the fence but the fence was not cooperating. Shit! they were right there walking right next to the fence directly towards me. I finally got through the fence just in time to have the first guy in the group stop and look right at me. I didn't turn my light on but the gig was up, LA MIGRA! Someone yelled. All hell broke loose, bodies busted everywhere. I was able to grab three of the guys that were in the front as the brush exploded all around me. There busting! I yelled on my radio. 10-4! An agent responded. I sat the three guys down next to the fence and turned my flash light on to make sure they were not armed. As I began to talk to the three subjects my flash light went dark. What the hell! I banged it on my hand. I twisted the top cover. Damn it! The bulb was probably burnt. "Hey guys my light is done, I'm on the fence line just start walking it south". I knew it would be a while before I got help so I just kept messing with my light. After the group had scattered, I knew they had not gone far because they did not continue to bust brush. I could now and then hear movement all around me not too far away. It was then I decided to try to use a tactic that would leer them towards me. It had been about ten minutes since I scattered them so I began to call out. "Pssssstt Hey come over here, we are right here, come here". "Pssst hey ven aqui estamos venance pa-ka, venance. Again, I repeated myself. Pssst come on we will leave right now before the BP gets here." Pssst venance orita nos vamos antes que llege la migra" I said all this in my best alien lingo. All of a sudden, I got a response. Psssst donde estan? Where are you? Someone whispered near me in

33

Spanish. "Aqui vente, I said." Donde? Where? Aqui! Here. We did this back and forth which helped the alien walk towards the sound of my voice. At this point I could hear the three guys I had apprehended laughing and beginning to get loud. Psst hey be quiet! I whispered. Umm no saben lo que les espera! Said one of the three. You do not know what awaits you. Then I could hear the brush breaking right next to me and a guy walked out of the darkness right to me. I grabbed him and told him to sit next to his friends. I continued to do this for a few more minutes and was able to get three more out of the group using this technique. Finally, no one answered my coaxing and I could hear agents calling my name at a distance. "I'm right here" I yelled as the brush broke near me. "Hey if you can hear my voice look around there should be more bodies near me". Agents arrived and ended up finding about nine more hiding in the brush around me. I ended up using this method whenever I could and it seemed to work. I give thanks to my native language which helped me deceive native speakers into my waiting hands.

SCOPE AT ZELLNER'S

In my career I became pretty good at just about everything, except scope operator. I knew the routes and the area and always found the groups but could never direct agents with the scope for shit. One night I get assigned to take a scope to Zellner's in Zone 28. I really didn't know where to set it up so I drove west from the station all the way to the scrapper passed Zellner's and turned around. On my way back on the border road I stopped on a high point on the west side of Zellner's. This location gave me a clear shot at the border fence and the gully trail. We called it the gully trail because there was a deep gully the aliens would run into just before they tried to cross highway 94. I set up the scope and began to scan for aliens near the fence. For a long while I didn't see anything. Eventually as I was scanning around, I finally got a glimpse of couple of guys near the fence right in the middle of Zellner's gully. Past practice was that if the scope operator observed something, he would advise the troops. Especially at Zellner's, it was about 100 yards to highway 94 and once they crossed the road, they were on their way to Hauser Mountain. I radioed "Hey guys I have three near the fence right now, I'll let you know if they go for it". There was no response. In those days there were large groups everywhere and three didn't[1] seem to be of any interest. I kept watching these guys, they would walk around look, north then south really not doing much. As I was watching them, I began to notice that a few more guys had joined them. "Ok guys there's about six or so now". "Ten For" I heard over the radio. It didn't seem that anyone cared. "Hey bro on my way, let me know," said an agent. "10-4" I responded. I took another look and now I could see a guy right on the fence. The guy would walk out to the middle of the border road and walk back south into Mexico. He did this a couple times. "Hey guys I think they're getting ready to cross, one guys keeps crossing the road and walking back". "Ok we're on our way" responded a couple agents. As I was watching the one dude hanging out at the fence, he motioned to another guy further south and all of a sudden, bodies! Everywhere, chingos of them!. "Hey guys what's your 20 (location) I have about 50 bodies getting ready to cross, right now!" Ok bro I'm getting close" responded an agent ". "I'm on highway 94 in the gully trail" responded another. "10-4, it looks like there beginning to cross I'll let you know if they go to Split Rock, Gully or M and M trail. "Their crossing! Chingos began to run straight north right towards the Gully trail. "The Gully trail, the Gully trail I called out". "They are headed straight for the gully trail". At this point the group had already made it half way across an open field and they kept crossing. "Hey guys there is a bunch, I can see them dropping into the gully and there are still more crossing the fence. The group was so big that the line of bodies started at the fence and continued all the way to the Gully trail 100 yards north. All of a sudden, bodies stared going everywhere, the straight line broke up and it looked like ants running around. I guess the agents had scattered the group in the gully and now all the aliens were trying to make it back south. It was hilarious watching them trying to make it back south, falling and stumbling and running into each other. I finally got could see agents coming out of the gully because they had their flash lights on. There were so many bodies that I was having a hell of a time trying to put agents in on them. "Can you see me!" "Can you see me!" is all you could hear on the radio. I was trying to stop laughing so I could answer them but I kept seeing aliens running towards agents, aliens falling, agents falling and no one apprehended. I regained my composure and finally tried to direct agents in on singles here and there but was unsuccessful. The group managed to all get back south and not body had crossed Hwy 94 which was pretty good considering the number. Well, that was a good lesson for me, I came to realize that I sucked on the scope and would try to get out if that as often as I could.

GROUP IN TREE JEWELL VALLEY

I was assigned to work Jewel Valley on this day. Artie and I had been working a group from the Dump Road heading towards Jewell Valley Road. These groups were notorious for laying up in rocks just north of the loop road on the east side. Artie had cut them (observed foot sign) crossing across the east side of the tracks access road. He began to follow the foot sign from there. I had been cutting north of him and cut them going across the loop road on the east side. "Hey bro I think I have them across the loop road heading east" 10-4 responded Artie. "I'll get out here and let you know" 10-4 responded Artie. I followed the foot sign and it was definite the group was heading for the rocks. "Hey bro looks like their headed for the rocks. "10-4" I knew that in a short time I would hear either I got them over here or habitus Corpus. Sure, enough I had not even got to the rock's yet when I heard "they're over here Toro", 10-4 I replied. "Hey bro I'll go grab my vehicle and meet up with you up ahead". "10-4!" I got back to my vehicle and started back on the loop road. As I was traveling north Artie kept me telling me where he was headed. He had reached the large meadow that is west of Jewel Valley Road. He reached a big oak tree that is located right next to Jewel Valley Road. I drove past the Caretaker's and could see Artie standing under a big oak tree not far from JVR. I got out of my vehicle and walked across the field and met up with him. "Hey Toro" I had them right here and I just can't figure out where they went from here. We both spent several minutes looking for the foot sign around the oak tree where we had them last. We both went on the east side of JVR to look for the foot sign but no luck. "I'm done," said Artie. By this time, it was late in the shift and it was time to head back to the barn (station). "Ok Bro" Ill head back in a minute, I'll see you back at the station. It was always in my nature to try and figure out where these aliens had gone. I back tracked the foot sign for a distance and started all over. The foot prints led me back to the tree and nowhere else. We both thought that they had tapped out or powdered out their foot sign. But where did they go? As I was staring down at the ground when I caught a little piece of a foot print at the base of the tree. The foot print was facing the tree right in the middle. But there was only the right foot print, but where was the left foot print. The tree was too wide for him to step around. At this point there could only be one place, straight up! I slowly looked up and there they were. All 15 of them spread all over the branches of the tree including some males and females. They all looked down at me with a defeated look as I began to tell them to come down. I called for transport and couldn't wait to get back to the station and tell Artie that I had found the group. Artie had been my journeymen and was the top dog at Campo station as far as I was concerned at apprehending aliens. I always will have the greatest respect for him, not only as an agent but as a person. I am proud to call him my friend.

EASY PICKINGS CONNECTOR RD

When I came in the Patrol in the early 90's there were no Field Training Officers. Junior agents would be assigned to journeymen to vehicle with them during the shift. On this night I was assigned to ride with Artie. Artie and Hector had decided to work together in Zone 27 near Tecate. It was expected That I would arrive ½ an hour early to work to get the vehicle cleaned and ready for the shift. I also made sure to ask the journeymen if he needed any other gear from the issue room. I asked Artie if he needed anything and he said no. We got into the Bronco and stared out. Artie pulled up next to Hector and said "The connector road ", "10-4 Hector replied". So, we went to zone 27 somewhere to some connector road. We got to the Connector Road and waited for Hector and his trainee to arrive. The Connector Road was a dirt road just south of the tire shop that connected with the G road in zone 27. The G Road ran from 4 corners all the way to Bell Valley just north of the city of Tecate. On the G road are these big electrical towers that are numbered, and we would use the numbers which we would use to identify a location. The tower numbers we used in this particular area began with #8 and ended at the #15 tower. This tower is on the west rim of Bell Valley. Directly south of this was the border fence about ½ a mile away. which in some areas went straight up. For some time, groups had been activating two sensors that were south of the connector road. One was situated by the nine tower and the other one was on a ridge by the Connector Road. This alerted us if the first sensor activated and the second one followed was a sure thing. Aliens would be passing right next to the pond adjacent to the connector road. We all got out of the vehicles and huddled up to make the plan. Of course, being the new guy, I just stood there listening and looking around in the pitch-black wondering what the hell I was doing there. Artie and Hector told us that we would be waking with out and laying in for group's that were coming through this area. We would all embed next to the trail about twenty feet apart and would let the group walk down the trail until the first guy in the group reached Hector the last guy in our gauntlet. Hector said once they stop get up quietly and calmly and sit them down on trial and "Don't turn on your lights! Being a nug it was a challenge trying to walk through an unknown area full of brush in the dark on a worn-down dirt path. It was kind of scary but exciting at the same time. We reached a spot where you could make out the top of a ridge and that's where we stopped. Artie and Hector had begun to whisper and said to take up positions on the trail about 20 feet apart from each other. "Let all the group get past the first guy and then the last agent will stop the group, lights out. "What?" I said to myself. Stop them with light's out! What if they have guns or knives? How can I see if they are armed? Now I'm getting scared. But I never would have showed it to my fellow agents. My fear became excitement, and I couldn't wait to see what happen. Well, sure enough the first sensor near the 9 towers, on the G road activated. Hector whispered "Ok boys there on their way". About ten minutes after a second sensor activated just above us on the ridge. This meant that the group would be in our area in about ten minutes. We all sat quietly waiting in the darkness for what we believed to be a large group walking to us. Then in the quiet of the night we heard the sound that would become a familiar and unmistakable sound of people walking through the brush. It was crazy to think these people were out here walking in the dark but yet here they were. Closer and closer the sound approached and at certain points I could hear the guide whispering in Spanish "Vamo nos! Vamosnos! callados!" "Go, Go, quietly". Soon they were close enough that we could tell it was a lot of people. heading our way. The closer they got the faster my heartbeat went up. At one point I thought they would be able to hear my heart; it was thumping so hard. I was positioned in the middle of our agents and could see the silhouette of a group of people walking on the trail. The trail was right next to us. The group were so close I could have reached out with my hand and tripped one of them. I let the group go past me and knew not to make a sound or get up until the group was stopped by the last agent in our line. Suddenly a voice broke the silence "Parense no se muevan" "Stop don't move" Hector said in a calm but commanding voice. The group stopped and we got up and began to sit them down with our lights off. "Sienten se, Sienten se" Sit down I whispered, as I grabbed each one and helped them sit down. It was crazy how they did not try to run. It was undoubtably because they did not know who we were and why we had stopped them. No one turned their flash lights on and there was no panic by anyone in the group. One by one we had them all on the ground. Once we had them I apprehended Hector turned his flashlight on and identified us as Border Patrol agents and told them in his calm voice to stay seated and not to move. At that point we all turned our flashlights on and waited for Hector to give us instructions. It was then that I could see that there was about 25 people including a couple woman. "Ok boys", Hector said "let's get these people out of here". We all began to walk back to the Connector Road and I could hear agents talking on the radio. "We are going to need transport on the north end of the Connector Road in about ten minutes" Hector said. Quietly we all walked the trail towards the road with only our journeyman using their flashlights, one in the front of the group and one at the end. Transport arrived and we loaded up all the aliens. "Hey bro keep your ears on, we will be calling you back" Hector said to transport. As the van drove away the pitch black of the night and silence returned, we all quietly began to walk on the trail to where we had embedded. I would never forget, how four agents could apprehend over seventy bodies and not endanger anyone.

59 IN A HOUSE

I was on a midnight shift and we were out and about patrolling the Border in Zone 30. At this point of my career there had developed cliques in our patrol group on the midnight shift. There were those that Had to be on midnight shift and those who Wanted to be on midnights shift. I enjoyed being a midnight guy. This particular night Randall and other agents had begun to work a group that had entered somewhere near Mesas Tree and was headed for Shasta and highway 94. As Randall and his crew worked the group Jessie and I were keeping track of the direction in which the group were heading. Recently these group would cross Insurance Road, walk the tracks head east towards Shasta. Eventually crossing over the east Indian road. The group would reach Shasta or go straight across and continue north. Eventually we heard Randall say that the group had crossed the east Indian heading towards Shasta. I radioed Jessie and told him that I was in the area and would look for the foot prints they were calling out. It didn't take me long to find the same group of footprints walking Shasta Road. I radioed Jessie and told him I had found the foot sign just short of highway 94 and would be tracking them on foot from this point. "10-4" he replied. "You have them on Shasta?" asked Randall. "Yea bro, they are on the road walking towards 94. "10-4" answered Randall in a discouraged tone. Soon after Jessie caught up to me and we both began to follow the foot sign towards highway 94. As we continued to follow the foot sign, we could tell it was a large group but didn't know how many. By this time other agents had gotten involved and were heading north to get in front of us. The group had made it to highway 94 but because it was now I pavement, we could not figure out what direction they had gone or where they had gone. Jessie decided to walk the edge of the road towards the north side and I started walking the edge of the road south. Jessie called out and said 'I have foot sign" found them crossing the road north of highway 94 and Shasta. I jumped to the side of highway 94 and came up on a long drive way that led in the direction that Jessie was headed. It was a sandy dirt road that I presumed was a drive way to a house. "Hey bro, you headed towards a house?". "Can't tell yet Bro I'm in the brush" answered Jessie." Ok "as I continued to walk up the long driveway. By this time the sun had begun to come up and we were able to see without our flashlights. I was walking up the drive way when I spotted a couple guys trying to hide on the top of a house that was at the end of the driveway. I noticed there were three vehicles parked in the drive way, two empty and one with two occupants. "Hey guys we need some units up here". We are just north of Shasta. I have bodies around this house and three vehicles in the drive way. By now we had units all over so it wasn't long before we had agents blocking the driveway as back up. "Hey Jessie, get up here bro, I think the bodies are in this house right in front of me. I waited for Jessie to arrive and we both went after the two guys hiding. It was odd that the two guys didn't run away from us but rather just stayed where I had seen them. Later I found out why. We rounded the two guys up and at that time Jessie told me that the foot sign was headed for the house. We both walked to the front of the house where we could see that someone had tried to rake the dirt to remove the foot sign in front of the door. We both looked at each other and at the same time said "they're in the house". By now Randall and his crew had arrived and surrounded the house. I knocked and listened to see if I could hear someone inside. I knocked again this a little harder "US Border Patrol open the door!' I yelled. I could hear sounds inside the house and I knew there were people inside. "Who is it?" a male voice answered "US Border Patrol open the door!' I yelled. "What do you want?" the voice replied. "We have been tracking a group from the Border and we believe that that they are in your house" I said. "There's no one in here" replied the voice. "Well, we have foot sign that led us to your front door!" We checked all around the house and there is no evidence of them continuing. There was no more dialogue it just stopped. "Ok I said we are not going anywhere until we figure out where these people are"! We have agents coming with a search warrant when it gets here, we will go in whether you like it or not!" I shouted. Time went by and now we could hear a lot of movement in the house. "Come on, let us in peacefully and we can get this over with" "Because once the warrant gets here, we will break this door down and get in the house anyway". "Ok, ok, ok, said the voice from inside. Slowly the door opened and instantly I could smell the pungent odor of bodies.

The voice that had been speaking to me was that of a short fat man. It appeared that he was a native American. As he stood there, I could see a group of people standing behind him. "How many people are in your house?" I asked. "Just me and my wife" answered the man. "OK, who are all those people standing right behind you?" "I don't Know" he answered. "What do you mean you don't know there are 10 guys right there!" At this point I entered the house and began to ask the aliens for their citizenship. They were all illegal aliens. By now agents that had been standing behind me began to enter the house to search. I went into an adjacent room and found about twenty bodies prone in the house. Other agents found more bodies in other rooms throughout the house. We had apprehended 59 individuals, 3 vehicles and two smuggler drivers. There was never a search warrant it was just a ruse to get them to open the door. We rounded everybody up and called the station to let them know what we had and to send transport. During the apprehension the Intel unit must have been listening to the radio because shortly after we called the Campo station they showed up. They were all excited and couldn't believe what we had found at this house. The Intel supervisor came up to me to ask if they could take the case from this point and I agreed. It was a midnight apprehension and it was time to go home. All that was asked of us was to help transport the bodies back to the station. "Are you Sure you don't need our help?" I asked the supervisor. "No, we got it from here good job". We transported the bodies back to the station and went home. The next day when I reported for duty the Field Operations Supervisor called me to his office and wanted to talk to me about the case. I was thinking he was going to give me a compliment instead he started chewing me out. "Why did you guys just leave yesterday and not help with the case? It was your case!?" "What? I said in an angry tone". I knew the supervisor on the Intel unit was kind of a jerk. I never imagined he would do me like that. "The Intel supervisor said that you guys just left and didn't help with case". "I told him twice before we left if he needed help and he had said that he would handle everything." I asked him if he was sure, and again volunteered to stay and help. He said "we got this "so we left. It turned out that they didn't process and complete the case and plus they gave the short fat man (principal) his guns back even though he was a felon. At any rate at least we got the 59 aliens and impounded three vehicles not a bad bust.

GROUP IN GREENHEAD

I remember once during winter it was cold as hell at the I-8 freeway checkpoint. Agents were all doing their rotations when (820) dispatch notified us that a sensor that was in a canyon in the area our check point had been activated. This canyon in Green Head, a shooting range west of the checkpoint. Brad and I were assigned to zone 55 (north of I-8 freeway) and immediately answered dispatch. Brad got on the radio and advised that he would go lay in (Lay in wait) on the trail and wait for the group. I told him I would stop by the check point and ask the supervisor if I could take a couple of agents with me. I stopped at the check point and picked up a couple guys and a van, just in case we needed transport. We all jumped in the van and drove into Green Head with our vehicles lights off. We did this all the time. I was very familiar with the road; it was no problem driving without lights. We got to where we usually parked our vehicles and three of us walked to our usual location. Brad at this point was laying north of us on the trail." Hey Brad we are here ready to lay in" I said in a low voice. "10-4 Brad" responded. Well, the sensor was a 30-to-45-minute walk to our location and I had positioned the agents in spots that would be perfect to apprehend the group. Tt was cold as hell and we had been laying on the cold ground for about an hour, "Brad 10-18, anything?" "Nothing yet" "10-4". I laid there for about another minute and got up. I told the agents "Change in plan". Big Q was one of the agents and I can't remember the other agent. Hey let's get the hell out of here and go sit in the van and warm up, "Fuck this", I said. Brad will stay in there all night and it won't faze him, I'm fucken freezing. All three of us got up and quietly walked back to the van. On I told the guys that if Brad called, we would have to get out of the van quietly and walked back to our positions lights out. We got in the van and no sooner had we begun to get warm I heard "Joe Copy?" in a whisper. This was a very familiar call from Brad that I had heard many times and I knew the group were coming. I told the guys, "Oh Shit!", they're coming we need to go back quietly with lights out. "If anything happens follow my lead". All three us started to walk back and we were about to turn a corner on the trail when we saw a group of 30 in front of us. I was in the front of the three of us and instantly I began to act as if I was lost." "Hey andamos perdidos! no hemos comido en tres dias! andamos perdidos!" Hey we are lost we haven't eaten for 3 days, we are lost, I said acting as if in a panic. I turned around and walked back and whispered to the agents start sitting them down and I will walk to the end of the group. I began to walk towards the back of the group repeating we were lost and hadn't eaten for 3 days. By now my eyes had adapted to the darkness and I could see the end of the line. At that point I began to sit the aliens down from the rear to the front as my partners did the same from the front to the rear. Eventually we had them all sitting on the ground without any noise or any of them trying to run away. We had begun to zip tie them when I could hear a person running down the trail. It was Brad running in the dark lights out. "Hey brad 10-15 (apprehended) bro" I said. "What the Fuck man I didn't hear shit man!" he said. "I know bro, we took them down quietly lights out, Oh and no golf". 10-4! We loaded them up and got the hell out of there.

CHE CHE GROUP IN CEDILLO

I was on the midnight shift and the swing shift had passed on a group that had crossed at the north end of Shockey and was heading east. The agents that were chasing them had lost the foot sign. The agents last location was on a two-track road on top of the ridge that parallels Shockey. The agents put me and my partner in area where they had stopped and we began to climb a ridge eastbound. At this particular time there was an organization that had a spotter (look out) that we called the "blanket dragger" He was really good at getting across roads without being detected. His tactic was to drag a blanket from the border to his final destination where he would load his groups. Later I found out he was guiding the groups and dragging the banket all the way to the 21-mile marker on MT Laguna. We got to the top of the ridge and I discovered that the guide had walked south and then crossed the two-track road. This led him into Cedillo Canyon. It was really crazy pushing(tracking) this guide. Because he would drag the blanket but now and then, he would leave a single foot print (a Vibram) on the trail. His intention was to make us think that it was an old group that had already been worked. To me it meant that it was one of Che Che's guides leading the group. We continued into the first small canyon to our east and started heading north. It came to a point where we continued north but realized we were no longer tracking sign. We turned around and started tracking south, one agent tracking the west side of the gully with me on the other side. I came to a point where I knew we were not tracking them. I began to look for anything that might indicate what direction they had taken. I looked around everywhere but was having a hard time finding any evidence. The only place that I had not focused on was a rocky ledge that I thought they would not have gone up. I began to look closer at the rocks when I saw on a small ledge a dirt area with a print on it. "I got them bro" I said to my partner. We both climbed the ridge and again began to follow the blanket drag. Suddenly there it was the Vibram shoe print on top of the drag on the trail.

I let the agents that had arrived to keep Cedillo hot and to check the road to make sure they had not crossed. "It's the blanket dragger boys, so be heads up". We continued and let the agents know that we were not too far from the east- west road in Cedillo. We continued towards the intersection in Cedillo when all of a sudden, the brush came alive. People started running in all directions. Luckily for us the area was loaded with Manzanita shrubs so the aliens were not able to run too far. This enabled us to round up 52 females and males that attempted to hide in the brush. We radioed to our partners that we had found the group and would be walking out towards the road. I let the group know that there was a scope on a nearby hill that was watching their movements and it would be impossible to get away. There was no scope, of course, but it seemed to work on occasions and it worked this time. As we walked out with the group agents began to help us bring them out to the road. We loaded all 52 bodies and I asked one of my partners who was operating a scope to set up just north of us. I advised him to set the scope in an area where he could see where we had scattered them. I wanted to see if there were any that hand been left behind. We cleared the area and later the scope spotted 10 more on the hill south of the road. A few agents were able to get 8 more. In all we apprehended 60 bodies that Che Che was trying to get to Mt. Laguna.

GROUP IN MT LAGUNA

We got the word that night from the swing that a group had been lost in Tulucks Wash heading towards Fred canyon. The last location of the group was climbing out of Tulucks Wash heading towards Troy canyon or Long Canyon. It had been raining on and off which made it harder to identify foot sign. I had a trainee riding with me that night so we began looking for the group. Recently were taking a route that would drop them into Troy or Long canyon heading towards Mt Laguna.

I decided to drive up Kitchen creek road past the bottom gate and check for foot prints in Troy canyon. There was a trail in the middle of the canyon used by groups. We stopped at Troy flats and walked the trail to the mouth of the canyon and it started raining. I knew if we were going to have a chance to find foot prints it had to be soon before the rain washed out the sign. The first main trail we checked had no sign, so we continued north to where I knew there was a barbwire fence line. We got to the fence and coming from the east was the foot sign of a group of about 20. They had come from Trulock's Wash crossed Fred Cayon Road and into Troy Canyon. This route was heading towards Mt Laguna and the Rodeo grounds. It was still raining and my sense of urgency grew by the minute.

We began to track the group and let agents know that we had found the group in Troy canyon. At first the tracking was good and the group stayed in the middle of the canyon. Unfortunately, there were no agents that night that knew this route or where the trail met the road in the rodeo grounds. I kept relaying that I was in the middle of the canyon for some time. My partner and I continued to track the sign in the rain and where still getting bits and pieces of sign, and getting soaked. As we continued up the canyon the rain became snow because of the elevation change. This made me feel lousy since I had a trainee, and the snow was starting to cover up the foot sign. Fortunately for us the group stayed in the middle of the canyon and at certain point we could still see faded divots in the snow that confirmed we were still on the chase. In some places it was hard to see the foot sign because it had not stopped snowing. About 2 hours into it, we finally started to see pine trees covered in snow and I knew the road was close. Upon reaching the road, we had the foot sign to the road but we couldn't figure out where they had gone. Damn! two-hour push and no foot sign and still no one in the area to assist us. I told my trainee "Lets split up and see if we can figure this out". This was a pretty big group and I couldn't see any foot sign on the road, but they had had plenty of time to erase crossing the road. We took a break and I remembered what an Old Journeymen had once told me, "If you ever lose the sign and are tired from a long push stop and regroup". I stopped and started looking around and noticed that on the main trail there were patches where the trees had not allowed the snow to cover the trail. I walked about 50 yards up the main trail and there they were on the trail heading north. I confirmed it was foot print, "I got them up here bro" I relayed to my partner. We started again but by now we were wet and very cold and had no radio communication. We stayed on the main trail and I knew that an old well was not too far off. As we crested over a small hill, we could see a glow in front of us. At first, I thought, "who would have a fire out here in the middle of nowhere". I never imagined what we were about to encounter. As we got closer, I could see silhouettes of a group standing around a really big fire. "Damn! that's the group bro I turned off my light and I immediately told my partner to stop and to turn off his flash light. I stood there for a bit trying to think of a plan. It was fucken freezing and we needed to get to that fire. I came up with the idea that we would act like we were lost cold and hungry and in need of help. I told my partner to follow my lead and to just go along with me. Since we were native speakers.

I told him to act as if we were arguing and to speak in Spanish only. As we got closer, to the group I began to talk in a load voice. "Te dije pinchi buey que no era por aqui!" I told you fucken idiot that this wasn't this way. My partner responded" Yo no te dije que te vinieras por aqui" I didn't tell you to come this way! "Es tu culpa buey!" It's your fault jackass! By now we were closer and I could see that a few of the people around the fire had heard us. "Hey mira alli estan unos paisas a ver sinos dejan arrimarnos ala lumbre" Hey there are some country men let's see if they will let us get near the fire. It was windy and freezing and by now all I wanted was to get next to that fire. As we got closer, I began to beg them "Por favor tenemos frio y nos vamos a morir si no nos dejan arrimarnos ala lumbe. Please we are cold and we are going to die if you don't let us near the fire. We were now close enough that I could see a guy wave us towards him saying "Vegansen aqui se pueden calentar" Come here you can warm up. We approached the fire and could feel the heat from this blazing fire. We both got into the circle that was surrounding the fire of 15 people. I got in between two of the illegal aliens and began to rub my hands together and blow into my fists. "Pinchi frio" Fucken Cold. We all stood there for about a minute and nobody said anything. The guy that was next to me looked at me once then looked back at the fire. Then all of a sudden, he looked at me again and then looked down towards my waist. My night sights on my pistol! I had covered them up when I got there but with me moving around, they had been exposed. "La Migra!" the man yelled in a loud voice. That was enough to scatter the group all over the place. They all ran in different directions into the darkness. "A donde van se van morir de frio si se pierden" I told them. I just stood there and continued to enjoy the warmth of the fire. A few of the aliens ran a few yards and stopped. Where are you going you are going to die from the cold if you get lost, I told them. We gathered up a few that had not run too far and we stayed by the fire as it began to get smaller by the minute. I started to yell to them in Spanish to those who had run into the darkness "The fire is going out and we will have to put it out before we leave so just walk back towards the fire. We stood there for a couple minutes and slowly the group started to come back towards the fire. We counted about 12 in custody and we knew that we were missing about 3 or 4. As we were all standing there, I asked one of the guys in the group how they had started the fire. He told me that they had wrapped the black plastic bags that they used to cover themselves in the rain, around the wood and started it with a lighter. Wow! It was resourceful how they could use stuff they already had to help them build such a big fire. As the fire began to burn out, we started to throw snow on top of it to put it out. "Ok we are leaving now and the fire is out if you stay you are going to freeze to death". "We already know you are here so just come out now". The wind had begun to pick up and it was time to leave. We started up the trail that I thought would lead us out of there. Not too far up the trail I noticed two divots heading up the trail. It was easy to see the divots in three feet of snow. I stopped the group and told my partner" Wait up bro let me check this out really quick and see if can find these knuckle heads". I knew that if I didn't find them this would turn into a rescue. If it wasn't already. I followed the divots for about 15 yards and under a very small pine tree was a pair hiding in the snow. "Get up its freezing out here and the fire is out". They both complied with my order and got up. It was a man and a woman.

Later we found out it was his wife. The man immediately began to tell me that his wife was not doing good. I shined my flashlight at her to take a better look and could see that her hands were swollen and were black and blue. "Oh shit!" It looked like she was starting to get frost bite and needed to get help soon. I got on the radio to see if my partners could get a bearing to where I was. Suddenly I heard a familiar voice. It was an old Campo journeyman that lived in the area and was familiar with Mt Laguna. "Flash copy?" (Do you read me) "Yea go ahead" he replied. I felt relieved that finally I could communicate and hear the radio clearly. "Hey give me a horn" I asked him. I could hear something but it sounded far off. Try again! Again, I heard a sound but it was faint. "Ok bro you are to my south", I'll keep going and try to get a bearing where I am. "10-4" We started up the trail again. As we moved forward, there were some spots where we could make out the trail and other spots where we couldn't. Not a good feeling. As we made our way up the trail the wind got stronger and the temperature dropped. It was pitch black, cold as hell and it was getting harder to stay on the trail. Shit! We continued to walk for about what seemed an hour and reached the top of a hill. At this point I was really starting to worry; everybody was following me and even I didn't know exactly where I was or which way to go. "Hang on bro" I told my partner. Let me go ahead a little bit and see if I recognize where I'm at". Just before that I had been thinking "should I go down into this valley or stay up high". It was dark as hell and I was getting nervous. I decided to keep going straight and hoping it was the right way. I had walked about 25 yards and could no longer see my partner's light. "Lord help me!" As I began to walk down a small slope, I caught a flash of light in my peripheral vision. "What is that?" I stood there for a second and again I saw a flash of light. The light got brighter and brighter until I could see that it was a snow plow. What a beautiful sight. Damn! I almost lost it and stated tearing up but had to keep my composure so that the others wouldn't think I was in trouble. I immediately radioed my partner that was already on the mountain and told him that I was able to see the 20mm sign on the road. "10- 4". I hurried back to the group and told them we were very close to the road and help was on the way. We had urgency in our step and got down to the road quickly. I notified my partner that we would need an EMT and fire department to evaluate one or more of the groups for frost bite. It did not take long for the fire department to arrive and a van was waiting to pick us up. We put the subjects in the van and all but one was doing pretty good considering what we had just experienced. It was the female that I had caught hiding with her husband that was not good. By now both of her hands were very swollen and she had begun to remove her jacket. These were signs of hyperthermia. Fortunately, the fire dept had arrived and began to render medical attention immediately. The woman's pants were so frozen that they decided not to cut them off and covered her with a bunch of blankets and prevented her from falling asleep. "Good job bro!" Flash said. "Yea that was gnarly bro let's get out of here. That was an adventure I will never forget and am thankful that things turned out the way they did.

RESCUE ON MT LAGUNA

On one occasion, I was Supervising the Strike team late in the swing shift around 11:00PM or 12:00 PM. We received a call I from dispatch. The sheriffs dept had requested assistance with two lost elderly people in Mt Laguna a mountain in East San Diego. The elderly couple and their two daughters had been camping in Mt Laguna. They had a camp site at a camp ground named Burnt Rancheria. This camp ground is located near Sunrise highway. According to the report the elderly couple had gone for a walk and had not returned for several hours. Fortunately for us, we were very familiar with this camp ground. The Pacific Crest Trail crossed on the side of the camp ground and was used by illegal aliens to go further north to load into vehicles. We arrived to the camp ground and noticed a bunch of vehicles in an area where the Sheriff had set up a command center. I told my agents to stand by while I found out what was going on. I approached the command center area that had been set up with large tents and tables and asked who was in charge. From the conversations that I had heard in the tent the agencies that were in charge of the operation placed their assets north. A search helicopter and several canine units been deployed to the north. I kept asking why they thought the couple were heading away from the camp ground. I was ignored by the command center personnel or maybe they didn't hear me when I asked them for clarification. Eventually I spoke to one of the sheriff deputies who explained to me what had happened. The deputy said that the elderly couple had last been seen walking north on a trail. The daughters also stated that they were expected back in a little while. The daughters were now concerned because their parents had been gone for several hours and it was now dark. The agents and I located the daughters sitting on a bench near their camp site. The two young ladies were very emotional and desperate to find their parents. I immediately began to try to comfort them by letting them know that we would find their parents. I explained to them that we knew the area better than probably anybody. I stated that we were very good trackers because that's what we did in our day-to-day work. I asked them where they had set up camp. They walked up a trail not far from the bench they had been sitting on and showed me. I looked the camp site over and noticed that there were two places where tents had been set up. I asked the girls about the arraignments of the tents. They told me that the tent up on the hill was the parents and the one below was theirs. "Our parents were the only ones walking around up next to the tent" said one of the girls. That immediately brought a smile to my face because I knew the only foot prints, I would find up there would be their parents. I walked up the hill on a dirt trail they had taken and could see that there were two sets of foot prints; a small print and a bigger one. I observed and identified the foot prints one was a running W and the other a bull's eye pattern. As I walked down the hill. I felt confident that we would find the elderly couple. It was just a matter of time. I said "I know we can find your parents; I know what their foot prints look like and we will track them". I asked them where they had last seen their parents and they pointed at a sign that was at the beginning of a trail. "Desert View, ok we will take it from here" I explained the foot sign to my partners and asked them to walk up the trail. I told them to let me know what direction the couple had gone when they reached the split in the trail. I told them that I would check the water fountain next to the Pacific Crest Trail.

To see if there were any clues what direction they had taken. By now it began to get colder and our sense of urgency increased. I reached the area and began to look carefully at the trying to identify the foot prints I had observed. Bam! There it was on top of everything, luckily no one had walked the trail and covered their tracks. By this time two other agents had arrived to the area. I got on the radio and let all the agents know that I had found the foot prints. I described them and explained that the foot prints were south bound. I instructed the agents that had just arrived at Mt Laguna to drive Thing Valley Road south. Check the road to the Cuyapaipe pump where the PCT crosses I told them I would go check Thing Valley Road about ½ south to see if they had crossed there. The PCT crosses over the road there and we could get a better idea where they were headed. As I reached my vehicle the two agents that driven told me that the foot sign was still on the PCT heading south. Great! As I drove Thing Valley Road, I observed a vehicle that was parked on the side of the. The PCT in this area runs next to the road so as I drove south, I was looking for my partners flashlights. "We are right here" they said "See our lights?" I turned and looked in my mirror and could see two agents walking on the PCT. "You got them there?" "Yes Sir" the agents replied. "Great stay on them". I sped up and drove down to where the PCT crosses the road and got out of my vehicle. The first thing I did was to look at the trail to see if the foot sign was still there. They were! I let all the agents know that the foot sign was still on the PCT. I began to follow the foot prints and realized that the elderly couple had crossed the road heading south. This wasn't a good thing. The PCT from this point heading south was very remote. There were several palaces they may have gotten off the trail. This would make it much harder for us to find them if they broke off the trail and wandered off into the forest. Shit! I got a little worried and continued to follow the foot sign. I crossed the road where they had stopped and had shuffled around. At this point they were probably thinking if they should either stay on the trail or turn back. The foot sign did not continue south so I took a closer look at them and realized that they had turned around and heading back to the road. Because I had walked on the trail, I inadvertently covered the foot prints. Now I was back on them and found the foot prints on the road continuing south. By this time the first two agents that had walked the Desert View trail had gotten mobile and I could see their headlights. I waited for them and was anxious to tell them I believed the couple were on the road heading south. "Hey Trujillo, they are on the road heading south bro" I said to the agent. Stay in your vehicle and just drive down the road checking every now and then to make sure they are still on the road. I knew that by doing this we could make up time. The couple would stay on the road and at some point, stop to rest. Trujjio and his partner drove the road as I waited for the two agents on foot to reach my vehicle. "Let me know as soon as you guys come up with something" I told them on the radio. As I was getting the two agents mobile, I received a call on the radio. "We found them!"

"10-4!" I called out. Where did you find them? They had walked the road south for quite a way until they reached cabins that are next to the road. "10-4! good job guys" I said. Trujillo continued to say that the elderly couple had walked to a point where they saw a cabin and walked up to see if it was occupied. After realizing that it was empty they decided to lay on a bench to rest waiting for help to arrive. "10-18 (what's happening) how are they doing?" I asked the agents. "They are ok just tired and cold and asking for water". "Ok 10-4" I knew that the agents had water because it was our practice to carry water. "We will get mobile and meet you back at the camp ground," said Trujillo. Trujillo and his partner made sure the elderly couple were ok to travel and headed back to the camp ground. I arrived at the camp site where the two daughters had been waiting and let them know that we had found their parents. "We found your mom and dad and they are ok and, on their way back, as we speak" I said. "What! the young ladies screamed" Oh my God! Thank You! Thank You! Thank you so much!" Yea we found them walking south they had stopped to rest at an old cabin. They should be here in a few minutes. Trujillo arrived after that and delivered the happy couple to their daughters. We decided that we would let the command center know that we had found the lost couple and that they were ok and back with their daughters. Because our service radios do not transmit on the same frequency as the other agencies that were involved, we were unable to let them know what we were doing as we were doing it. Trujillo and I entered command center and there was still a ruckus going on. People were looking at maps and talking about what areas they had searched in and what the next plan of action would be. "Sir, Sir" I tried to break into the conversation but the ruckus was too loud. At that point agent Trujillo tapped one of the guys on the shoulder and said "We found them sir!" the man turned and said "What?". And at the same time Trujillo and I both said "we found them!" At that point the man began to scratch his head and asked us where we had found them. "They were headed south on the Pacific Crest Trail" I said. It was quite a sight to see the and hear the command center become quiet. Everyone seemed to be in disbelief and stood around looking at us as if we had ruined their show. It was a great feeling to use our abilities to help someone in need and the agents involved did an outstanding job. We located the lost couple in about an hour using our leap frog method and our familiarity of the area. Tracking is a skill we used daily and some of the best trackers have come from the Campo Border Patrol Station.

WHERE DID THEY GO?

I remember I it was during the winter on midnight shift because it was cold as hell and it had been snowing. Dispatch informed us that a sensor had been repeatedly activated in the Mount Laguna area and had taken several hits. I acknowledged the sensor activation and headed towards the mountain. Artie got on the radio and said he would meet me there so we could work together. We both drove down the end of the Cuyapaipe pump road and exited our vehicles. "Hey "Artie, what do you think, lay in for a while and see if they show up?" I spoke. "Oh Yeeeaaa Toro" Artie said. It usually took the group a while to get to the spot where we were going to lay in so we had plenty of time. We both headed down the trail to set up for the group. "I'll let them pass me and you stop them Toro," said Artie. 10 -4 I replied. In this type of lay in agents find a spot next to the trail and hunker down. One agent stays in the front and one in the rear separated by about 20 yards. The front agent lets the group walk by him until he hears the agent in the back stop the group. This is all done with lights out and quietly. They should be here pretty soon. The sensor had activated in plenty of time for us to both find comfortable spot. We both found a spot on the side of the trail with about 15 yards between us. It was very cold and Fucken dark that night and could hear everything around you. We sat there for about 15 minutes which seemed to an eternity because it was so cold and dark. Then off in the distance I could hear the sound of people walking. "Here they come Artie" I whispered. 10-4. Arite replied. The sound got louder and we knew they would be to us in just a little bit. Suddenly the sound stopped and we couldn't hear them anymore. We both stayed really quiet and waited to see if they sent someone up ahead. We waited and waited and couldn't hear any movement. We waited for about another 15-20 minutes and never heard them again. "Toro, Toro" Artie whispered" let's go look for these guys its Fucken freezing. "10-4 bro". We both started down the main trail cupping our flashlights looking down to avoid taking a spill. We reached an old wire gap and decided to turn our lights on. I thought that had they made it to this point. We both looked at each other and shrugged our shoulders. "Let's go find these guys". We slowly began to walk the trail checking carefully to make sure they didn't break off somewhere. It was really cold and some of the snow had become ice so it made it really hard to see any foot prints. "Hey bro lets walk the trail and see how many we are looking for; the road will be covered with snow and we should see something" I said. We continued to walk the trail and check carefully until we reached the road. Oh shit! There was nothing on the road but snow. Everywhere we walked we were leaving foot prints but there was no sign of anybody else. We both started to get a bad feeling. "You heard them right Artie?" "Yes". "Shit man what the Fuck!" Let's walk up the trail and make sure they didn't come in from another direction. So, we walked back up the trail hoping to find them coming in on the trail from any other direction. Eventually we reached the wire gap again with no sign of a group in the area. At that point we both looked at each other and said "Let's get the Fuck out of here" We both made our way back to the vehicles and never said a word. "What do you think Bro?" Unidentified 10-4! Until this day whenever I see Arite I ask him Hey bro you heard them that night, right? "Yes sir!" Luckly we were there as witnesses and can tell our tale to other agents. What a night. Where did they go?

DAMN ITS COLD!

We had been experiencing groups coming up Potrero Canyon from the desert and had not made many apprehensions. We initially placed a sensor at the base the canyon but could never figure out when the groups would reach the top. Sometimes we would lay in and they wouldn't show up. Then later we would check the top of the canyon and find them out waking for the PCT. Eventually Brad and I placed a sensor on the top of the canyon where it narrows and turns into a gully. Potrero canyon is south of the Desert View Road and stops at the Mt Laguna overlook south of the Doppler. Potrero canyon dumps into the desert at zero elevation in a large wash. Groups would start in the desert and make their way up the canyon towards Mt Laguna where they would get picked up by smugglers at several points along the road. On this particular day the Swings shift Strike team acknowledged the sensor activation in the desert and headed up towards Mt laguna. It was still day light so we would have enough time to set and perhaps spot the group coming up the canyon. On the way up a couple of intel agents called us and advised us that they would be in the area to assist us. 10-4! We passed the General store and just past the Community church on the north side or the road. We drove into the driveway of a cabin. I backed into the drive way to avoid smuggler scout vehicles that might drive by. "Ok boys this the plan" I said to the agents. We will walk down the main trail in the gulley and see if we can spot anything coming up." the trail. I had walked this trail many times and already had a spot where I knew we were going to lay in for the group. Just short of the edge of the canyon where the canyon drops straight down there was a large bush. The trail the aliens used had a big bush in the middle it which made a perfect spot for us to apprehend the group. We would wait until the group emerged from the bush and apprehend them as they came out of it. That is where I told the agents to stand by while I used my binoculars. I wanted to see if any aliens were coming up the canyon. I got to the edge of the gully and looked down. At the bottom of the canyon 7 aliens were making their way up. I got really excited because that was the first time, I had observed people walking up towards our location. I walked back to the agents that were with me and told them that the group was on the way up. I told them that I had seen them. I decided that two agents would lay in on opposite sides of the bush. One agent would walk the trail south where the bush began and lay in just a little bit off the trail. That agent would let them walk by and let them commit to entering the bush before he would begin to follow. The rest of us would wait until the front of the group stared to come out of the bush and we would apprehend them. It had been snowing the ground was covered in snow and it was really cold. When we first arrived to the area it was still light but soon it would be dark which would be and better for us. Either way we would be waiting for them. I remember thinking as it began to get dark, "man it's going to get Fucken cold up here". We all found a spot we could hide in and hunkered down. I found a spot under a bush and could see my partner straight across from me. Perfect! My partner was just north of both of us hiding behind a tree. We waited and waited and waited but the group didn't come up. We had been there laid in since I spotted them earlier. Two or three hours had gone by and it was getting colder and colder. Especially since were just lying there not moving in the snow. At a certain point I couldn't feel my hands, my feet were numb and I knew the rest of the agents were probably in the same condition. "Fuck This! "I whispered to the agents lets go back to the truck and worm up, we can come back after we, warm up. 10-4! We made our way out it was about a ten-minute walk to the PCT and Desert View Road. Eventually we got back to the vehicle and in the truck to warm up. Fuck we were freezing. "Ok, guys this the plan: if the sensor activates, we need to hall ass back to the PCT trail and lay in at the first sharp bend in the trail. There is no way we can make it back to where we were. We will need to get there quick, lights out and hope we have enough time. We probably sat there for about five minutes and Bang! The sensor goes off. Shit! There they are! Let's go boys! We all jumped out of the vehicle and headed for the PCT trail. We ran up Desert View Road and south down the trail. It was pitch black and super quiet as we ran up the road lights out. "OK, we will spread out on the trail one on the south side one in the middle and one to stop the group I whispered"

We all started looking for good spots to lay in, when off in the distance I heard them. Damn! They are walking towards us! I spoke. At that point I notified the two intel agents that I would let them know when to walk down the PCT to help us. 10-4! They responded. We had just settled in, and we could hear the aliens getting closer and closer. Because it had snowed and there was ice here and there, it was easy to hear them walking. It also gave us an idea of how close they were to us. They had reached the trail because you could no longer hear the snow or the ice cracking. As your laying there your heart beat increases and you are like a cat waiting to pounce on a mouse. Now they were getting close we could hear them walking on the trail just short of where we were waiting. I was in the middle and they were just away from me. As we prepared to execute the ambush, I could hear footsteps coming down the trail towards us. Damn! It was the two agents that had been mobile and were now out on foot heading towards us and the group. There wasn't time to radio them or even to try to whisper to them, the group was too close. I laid there, heart pounding, slowly I began to see silhouettes of bodies walking on the trail next to me. Two of the aliens there had just walked by me when all of a sudden, they stopped. The two agents had walked down the trail and were now right in front of the group lights out. The agents thought that the group was us and at that point turned their lights on. Everybody jumped up and tried to grab as many aliens as possible. The alien that was in the front of the group turned and ran and managed to bust into the thick brush. The alien that was in the back also managed to get away and ran down the main trail back south. We were able to apprehend 5 out of seven in the group. The alien that was in the front busted through the thick brush. We never found him. The alien that was in the rear later hit the sensor on his way back south towards the desert. Gulf! We all regrouped and figured 5 was better than zero and we knew that the two that got away (Gulf) were the guides. Overall, it was a successful operation, no one got hurt and we got 5 out of 7. Our time freezing our asses off had paid off and it was quite an adventure.

LIGHT ON THE TRAIL

Brad and I were on midnight shift and had responded to a sensor activation in Mt Laguna. "10-4 820 ". As we headed up the mountain, we heard a familiar voice call out" hey guys I'm heading that way too ". 10-4 we responded. It was agent Shawn. We all met up at the wire gap that is on Sunrise Highway near the 21-mile marker. This wire gap gate opens to a road that takes you to the rodeo grounds where we were headed. The plan was that we would lay in just north of the sensor on the trail that came out of Troy canyon. No sooner had we arrived when a thick layer of fog began to fill the area. We all got together to talk about how we would set up. Because I was the Spanish speaker, I would stop the group as soon as it got to me. "Ok" I'll stop them and you guys just let them walk by" I said to Brad and Shawn. "Hey Joe, let me stop them this time" Brad said.

Brad never stopped the groups; he always was the guy in the back of the group walking right behind them. "How funny!" "Ok Brad" you got it! So that meant that Shawn and I would be the two agents to let them walk by and fall in behind until Brad stopped them.

Usually, it took the group about 30 minutes to get to the point where we would be waiting for them. But because it was really foggy that night it was taking them a little longer. We all settled in our designated spots, I was the first agent Shawn was in the middle and Brad was going to stop the group. As we walked down the trail Shawn and I were laughing because we had never heard Brad stop a group and didn't know what to expect. I was about 20 feet from Shawn and we were both lying just off the trail. We were so close you could touch the group as they walked by. Suddenly off in the distance we heard people walking up a rocky trail heading towards us. It's crazy, your heart begins to beat rapidly and your adrenaline hits the roof. I sat there quietly as the group got closer and closer. As they got closer, I could hear whispers but could not make out what was said. Now I could hear a guy clearly. It was the guide telling the group to keep up and stay next to him. As he got closer, I could see a faint light now and then. "What the hell?" I thought to myself. As he got closer, I could see what he was doing. He was using his cell phone as a light to stay on the trail. He would bend over to get the light low to see the trail or maybe to see any boot sign. As I sat there all I could think of was "man I hope this guy doesn't see me". That's how close I was to the trail; I could have touched him when he walked by. At this point the guide had walked past me and was heading towards Brad. Several bodies had walked by me and the last couple of stragglers were next to me. I was wondering where Brad had set up because we hadn't heard anything and the group hadn't stopped moving. In the dense fog pitch black night, you heard "Stop Bitch!" it was Brad. Aliens started Scattering everywhere! I grabbed a few next to me and sat them down in the middle of the trail to stop them from running back south. Shawn jumped up ran about 20 feet and fell and sprained his ankle. Brad sat 10 that stayed on the trail and I stopped 7 on the trail. Shawn eventually made his way back to the trail agonizing in pain and disappointed that not only had he not apprehended any alien but had sprained his ankle. We gathered up the aliens, walked them up the trail and sat them next to our vehicles. "Well, that was exciting" I said as I began to bust up about what had just happened. We all stood around for a while laughing and talking shit waiting for more transport. As I stood there, I realized what we had accomplished and how great it was to work with guys like Brad and Shawn. Not everybody likes to do or what we do at night. Oh and of course "Fucken Brad!"

WHO'S TO GUIDE

During a midnight shift a sensor was activated in the narrows in Kitchen Valley. Kitchen valley is on the west side of Kitchen Creek Road west the Troy Flats. This sensor was for groups that would travel through Kitchen creek road. The trail was an old fire break that led to Kitchen Valley. The trail parallel Kitchen creek road in a narrow canyon. One sensor was on the end of the trial where groups would walk north. The trail led to the road in Kitchen Valley which was about a half a mile away. The secondary sensor was also located near the road. Usually, the first sensor would activate and this gave agents plenty of time to head north. This particular night the sensor activated and it was confirmed by agents that there were foot prints in the area. There were ten in this group heading up the trail. I acknowledged the agents checking the sensor and advised that I was in route to work it. Another agent heard me and called to let me know that he and a trainee where also in route to assist me. I called them on the radio and asked them to meet me at the Sheep Head gate on Kitchen creek road. This gate opened to a road that was not drivable. It would take us a while to walk down Sheep head road where two roads connected. We got to the gate and I explained to Woody and his trainee what we would need to do. We would walk the road until we reached the point where the roads connected and wait for the group. Most of the road was no longer there and it was a 15 min walk to the junction. We reached the spot where the roads connected and walked the road a small distance south. This road continued north towards some corals in Kouches Meadow. The groups would continue on until they reached Sunrise highway near the Moo tanks where they would load into vehicles. I cupped my flashlight and put it low to the ground to see if they had reached this point but there were foot prints. "It was on!" Mt laguna at night is really dark especially with all the tree cover and no ambient light. "Ok, here's the plan" I said I need one agent to set up one on the side of the road and one in the middle on the opposite side of the road. I will stop the group when they reach me and you guys will pop out when you see them sit. I will have them sit lights out and you guys can turn your lights on when I do". The plan was set. I was wearing a camouflage jacket and a black beanie. I hid behind a large pine tree that was right next to the road. We waited about 20 minutes and we began to hear people walking at a distance heading towards us. The sound got louder and louder and I could hear them coming getting closer. I could now see dark silhouettes of a group of people walking in file down the round towards us. I knew that the first person in line would be the guide because he knew the way. As the first person got close to me, I stepped out from behind the tree, lights out. I grabbed him by his shoulder and said "Parate buey, La Migra esta ahi adelante, calmate" Stop dude the border patrol is up ahead, calm down. "Quien eres Tu? Who are you? "The guide asked. "Soy guia buey calmate "Im a guide dude calm down. I grabbed him firmly and walked him back to the group and sat him down. "Sienten se, cienten se" sit down sit down I said to the group. The group began to it down after they realized the guide had done the same with a bit of assistance. At that point I turned my light on and the two other agents jumped out and secured the aliens. Now the group knew what had happened and were sitting there waiting to be searched. I had the guides collar and passed him over to the trainee to keep an eye on him. I wanted to walk down the trail to make sure we had apprehended all of them. I took a few steps down the road and suddenly heard a commotion behind me. "Stop! Stop! Stop! The trainee yelled in a loud and panicked voice. I turned to see Woody running on the side of the hill yelling Stop! Bitch! "It's the guide!". The trainee yelled as he ran down the road trying to cut him off. I watched Woody try to catch up to him but that was not going to happen. These guides do this for living and are the most fit people you will ever encounter. Soon after I got on the radio and called Woody. "10-3 bro he's gone don't worry about him we got his group" I said. Woody and the trainee regrouped and had a conversation about what had happened. The Trainee said that he had sat the guide down at the end of the line when he jumped on his feet and took off. It's really interesting how the guides know or sense when trainee agents don't have the experience or officer presence that journeyman agents have. I know this from experience as you have read from other events I have described. Woody and I talked to the trainee and explained to him what he needed to change and left it at that. We walked the group back up to road and drove them in for processing.

52 ON THE TRACKS

It was another midnight shift and we were at the old station in Campo. Campo was getting killed by large groups everywhere in our area of responsibility. That night a sensor activated near the border near Mesa's Tree. This sensor was very reliable detecting incursions. At that time, we were mustering up 8 agents to patrol 30 miles of border. The majority of the groups that activated that sensor at that time were heading straight north from Mesa's tree to the Insurance cut. Once on the tracks they would stay on them to the high Tressel. I got on the radio and acknowledged the sensor "10-4" 820 I said. Soon after I asked if anyone was available to give me a hand. One agent answered up. "10-18" the agent said. "Hey bro I'm going to head up to the Center cut and lay in to see if its good I'll let you know if you want to get north of me" I said. Or you can meet me there. "10-4 I'll be on 94 highway) the agent responded. I thought what the hell! The group wouldn't get there for about another hour! Oh OK! I didn't go to the sensor because it had activated and I wasn't in the area. I was on the West Indian driving south when the sensor hit. I went lights out as soon as I got close to the Center cut and drove slowly eastbound. I knew the area pretty well so I drove to a point where I could get out and walk without being heard or seen by the group. I reached the tracks and knew I had some time so I found a good spot at the end of a small cut bank. The radio was quiet no traffic at all, the agent who had agreed to help me was nowhere to be found. As I lay there, I heard the tracks snapping. This was a sign that the group were coming so I got ready to act. I turned my radio off just to make sure the group wouldn't get spooked. About 15 minutes later I could hear in the distance people walking in the middle of the tracks. Shit! It was getting louder and it sounded like it was a bunch of them. Now my heart was racing and my adrenaline was sky high. By now my eyes had become adapted to the dark and I could see and hear a dark row of people heading towards me on the tracks. As they got closer, I noticed that they were making a lot of noise walking on the tracks. This usually meant that there was a lot of people. Now they were right there, next to me on the tracks. I sat there quietly and watched as the silhouettes of the people walked past me one after another. Damn! It was a bunch of them! I sat there for what seemed an eternity and finally the last of the group passed my location and continued north on the tracks. I let them get across and waited another 5 minutes so that I could get back to my vehicle without them hearing me. From the Center cut to the high trestle it usually took 20-30 minutes for groups to walk there. I knew I had time to drive back to the tracks access road. This road gave me access to the tracks on the east side. I gave the group a little more time as I walked to my vehicle and thought about what I was going to do. Damn! It was a shitload of them! I got on the radio and advised agents that I would be heading to the high trestle and if anyone was available. "Come in lights out and meet me on the tracks" I said. Only one agent answered, it was the same agent I had spoken to earlier. "I'll be on highway 94" he answered up. Shit! I realized I was on my own! I drove lights out and headed up the access road traversing the shitty part of the road. I got out of the vehicle and closed the door quietly. It was dark and quite perfect for a lay in. Fortunately for me at the tracks where the road intersects there was a large cut bank about 100 yards long. The high trestle was about 100 yards north. The sides of the cut bank are 30 to 40 feet high and there was no way you could crawl out once you were in it. This is where I would wait for the group in order to trap them in between the bank. Since I was alone, I would have to improvise to apprehend the group. I got to the tracks and walked it in lights out about 20 yards. I didn't wait long. I could hear them coming, damn! I made sure my radio was off and I crouched against the bank. As the first guy in the group approached, I walked up slowly, stopped him and quietly sat him down. Sientate Senate, sit, sit I whispered. The rest of the group followed him and sat down. I couldn't believe it! Slowly I made my way down the group sitting more people down. Damn! I realized the group didn't end and I was getting too far from the front of the group. Most of the group was sitting except for a few in the in the back. I turned on my flashlight and immediately began flashing it as if I was signaling agents to my south. "No se muenvan estan rodiados! Don't move you are surrounded" I said in a commanding voice. At the same time, I acted as if I were on the radio talking to agents that were approaching me. "Hey I'm right here, see my light" I said as I waved my flashlight back and forth. I continued to do this until I felt the group understood they were trapped in the bank. Fortunately, at that exact moment a light flew across the sky, "miren, alli esta el helicoptero ", "look there's the helicopter" I said as I pointed up towards the light. Once I realized that the group was not going to bust (scatter) and no one was trying to get up I got on the radio. Hey, does anybody copy I have bodies on the tracks, south of the high trestle. "10-4 how many do you have ten fifteen (in custody)?" "I don't know but there is a bunch".

"Somebody drive the tracks access road and stop at the south end of the last big cut bank." Get out and start walking on the tracks I'm on the north end of the bank. A few minutes later I could see an agent's flashlight towards me. "Right here bro" I said as I flashed my light so he could see my location. It was at this point that I began to feel better about being there with this size group alone. Not long after that the Campo station called and asked if I needed transport and how many we had 10-15 (in custody). I said I'll let you know as soon as my partner gets to me, stand by". I don't recall who it was that walked in but as soon as he arrived, he said Damn! Bro!" "How many you got here?" "I don't know bro lets count them". "I'll start from the front and you start from back and we will meet in the middle". As we walked toward each other I started to realize how big this group was. 52 was the final count. Damn! Bro! Good bone! I called the station and let them know that we had fifty-two on the ground. "10-4" the station replied. While we were waiting one of the guys in the group asked if they could eat. "Si como no, coman" "sure go ahead and eat" I replied. I told them that once we get back to the station, they would not be able to eat the food they had brought. It was interesting because at that moment I realized that this group was without a guide and that's why they had not all scattered when I stopped them. How lucky can you get! The whole group sat and began to eat their food while we waited for transport to arrive. Transport arrived and all the aliens were taken back to the station for further processing.

LEAVING MY POST

One night I was assigned as checkpoint supervisor and was listening to communications over the radio. Agent Quintero was assigned a mobile infra-red scope and was patrolling the area. While in Zone 30 agent Quintero observed three suspects crossing the border. The subjects were heading in the directions the 6-mile maker on Tierra del Sol. He notified the agents and explained their movements and direction of travel. Looks like the group is headed towards Tierra Estrella. They are walking the access road from TDS" Q said. '10-4" agents responded. Agents advised that they were in the area. "Be advised it looks like these guys are carrying title 21(Duffle bags full of contraband) so heads up" Q said 10-4! Agents responded. "They are getting really close to Tierra Estrella "Q said. "Ok we are on Tierra Estrella Q, let us know" agents responded. "Ok they are crossing the road! There is an agent right next to them, I don't know what he is waiting for!" Agents arrived to the location and began to look for foot prints. "That is where they crossed". Ok I can't see them anymore but they did cross the road. "10-4" agents replied. A few minutes later Q was on the radio, "ok I have them breaking west". "Ok I can see agents behind them stay on that line". Just so you know they are not caring the bags Q said. Somebody needs to go back and look for the bags Q explained. Ok Q we can hear them right in front of us agents replied. "10-4 but somebody needs to go back and look for the bags! Q stated". 10-4 I'm where they crossed Q. 10-4. Meanwhile I was sitting at the checkpoint listening. I sat there anxiously expecting a better outcome. I couldn't wait any longer. "10-18 (What is going on) did anybody go look for the bags" I said. "No sir" responded an agent. At that point I made the decision to leave the checkpoint. "Hey Q I'm 13 (in route) from the checkpoint". 10-4 Q responded. I drove my vehicle to the border area where the agents were working. I expected to hear someone had located the bags so I could head back to the checkpoint. I drove Tierra Del Sol towards Browns corner and began to drive west." Ok Q I'm in the area ". I drove about 25 yards and stopped my vehicle and I could see the silhouette of a person standing in the middle of the road. He was looking at the ground with his flashlight low to the ground. Meanwhile the other agents were still chasing the three suspects' heading back to Mexico. I walked to the agent and asked him. "10-18 bro?" (what's going on) The first thing he said was, "they crossed right here". "Where?" I asked. Right here, I saw them." Yeah, they crossed right here. I just can't figure out where they went the agent whispered. "Ok well let's get on the foot sign, it was booties, (cloth wrapped around shoes to avoid leaving foot prints) and figure this out" I said. The agent showed me the last place could see sign. "They are here and it looks like they are heading west" he said. "Ok let's look around" I said. The agent began to walk across the road and I followed him. He continued and there was a point where I couldn't see any scuff marks. What was he looking at? I stopped and backtracked and noticed that there was some disturbance in the soil heading towards a small gully. I dropped into the wash and walked a short distance. I could see a couple places where someone had left divots in the sand. "Hey bro I think I have them over here" I yelled. "Ok Sir". "Hey Q I have the booties in the wash bro". 10-4 Q answered. We followed the divots in the wash another 30 yards and around a bend there were three duffle bags. "I found the bags Q". 10-4 Q answered. "How many do you have?" Q asked. I saw three bags. "Three bro!" I replied 10-4 Q said. All the agents working the area arrived where the bags were found. It turned out that the bags were found next to my vehicle where I had stopped! Good job Q! I said 10-4 Q responded. I asked the agents to take the title 21 (Narcotics) back to the station and informed them I was returning to the checkpoint. I would do my documentation for the contraband at the checkpoint and would assist them when I was relieved. The contraband was possessed and stored as evidence. My concern was that I had left the checkpoint. I didn't know how the Patrol Agent in Charge would react to my decision. At the end of shift I was sitting at my desk waiting to be dismissed. The PAIC walked past my office, Oh, shit! I thought, is he looking for me? He walked just past my office turned back and stuck his head in the doorway. "Hey Joe, did you get that dope last night?" "Yes Sir", I answered. "Good job, just over 200 pounds, right?" Yes sir! That was extent of our conversation and I never heard another word about leaving the checkpoint. In my opinion he is the best PAIC Campo ever had. It felt good to be able to help and accomplish the mission with no repercussions.

NORTH AND SOUTH

On one occasion, I was working on Swing shift and was scheduled to work in Zone 29 the entire week. I had been driving the border road daily looking for foot prints crossing the road. During one of my cuts (checking the road for crossings) I observed the same foot prints entering in one particular location from the border and retuning back to Mexico in separate areas. This was an indication and raised my suspicion that there was something being dropped off somewhere north. Returning back to Mexico in different locations was a tactic used by smugglers to avoid detection. While investigating an area on the border road where a large rock was exposed, I made an observation. The rock extended over half of the dirt road and made it easy to cross and not be detected (147 tower). In addition, the angle of the ground forced the drag (tires drug to clean the surface of the road) to clean only the dirt portion of the road.

As I drove this section of the road, I observed a small path coming onto the rock. I exited my vehicle to investigate and could see broken brush and foot prints coming from the path. I walked across the rock and noticed that from the edge of the rock to the other side of the road was a short distance. This would facilitate throwing bags over the road without detection. I continued to investigate and observed square imprints left by duffle bags. These imprints had been left by heavy military style duffle bags filled with narcotics. This confirmed that narcotics were being smuggled on this trail. I followed the foot prints for a distance and discovered the canyon they were using to head north (149 wash). I decided I would try to find the foot prints I had observed further north. Eventually I found the route the group was taking and explained the route of travel to agent Ramos. I explained to him if a senor activated in the wash, he should check the rock to confirm an entry. I would go to the area where I had found the foot prints up north and wait for the group. Later in the shift there was a sensor activation in the wash. "Hey Ramos you copy that?" I asked. "10-4" replied agent Ramos. It was not long before agents Ramos advised that it was good traffic. I asked another agent for assistance and explained that I knew the route the group was taking. He explained to me that he believed he knew the route the group was taking. I was left no option but to go into Far Valley alone. It was scary going where I knew eight subjects with contraband were heading. I drove into the back of Far Valley (church of God) lights out and parked my vehicle. It was dark and quiet. I walked a path that led me into a deep gully. I cupped flash light and pointed towards the ground to check for foot prints. There was no evidence of recent foot prints in the gully. I could hear agent Ramos advise he was following the foot prints heading towards me. Eventually I walked out of the gully and was on a path. Suddenly I heard the sound of people walking and clothes rubbing on brush. I concealed myself behind a large bush that was next to the path. I was having a hard time distinguishing weather the sound was coming towards me or moving away. I crouched with my weapon in hand and listened.

Usually, smugglers that are transporting contraband are armed and I wasn't going to take any chances. At a point I realized the sound was moving away from me. I tuned up my radio and advised agent Ramos that the group had reach my location and was scattering back south. I turned on my flash light and walked a few steps and on the other side of the bush next to the trail were four large duffle bags. "Hey Ramos I have bags!) I yelled. By this time, I could hear agents approaching. I continued to search and found two more bags. The agent's arrived to my location and we secured the area. An attempt was made to locate the smugglers with a helicopter but no people were apprehended. I notified a supervisor in the area of what had transpired and asked for assistance. The supervisor arrived and was in disbelief that I had gone in alone to intercept the group. We carried out the 480lbs of contraband to the vehicles and transported it back to the station. It wasn't until later that I realized what had transpired. I had hidden behind a bush where minutes earlier a group of ten smugglers possibly armed watched me walk towards them. That night I realized the courage I had and felt proud to be a Border Patrol agent.

Volume two coming soon!

Printed in the United States
by Baker & Taylor Publisher Services